# THE ENTREPRENEURIAL COLLEGE PRESIDENT

# THE
# ENTREPRENEURIAL
# COLLEGE PRESIDENT

James L. Fisher and James V. Koch

Foreword by Gene A. Budig

AMERICAN COUNCIL ON EDUCATION
PRAEGER
Series on Higher Education

Library of Congress Cataloging-in-Publication Data

Fisher, James L. (James Lee), 1931–
  The entrepreneurial college president / James L. Fisher
  and James V. Koch ; foreword by Gene A. Budig.
    p. cm.—(ACE/Praeger series on higher education)
  Includes bibliographical references and index.
  ISBN 0–275–98122–3
  1. College presidents—United States—Attitudes—Case studies. 2.
Education, Higher—United States—Finance—Case studies. I. Koch, James V.,
1942– II. Title. III. Series. American Council on Education/Praeger series on
higher education.
LB2341.F495 2004
378.1'11—dc22          2004003817

British Library Cataloguing in Publication Data is available.

Library of Congress Catalog Card Number: 2004003817
ISBN: 0–275–98122–3

First published in 2004

Praeger Publishers, 88 Post Road West, Westport, CT 06881
An imprint of Greenwood Publishing Group, Inc.
www.praeger.com

Printed in the United States of America

The paper used in this book complies with the
Permanent Paper Standard issued by the National
Information Standards Organization (Z39.48–1984).

10  9  8  7  6  5  4  3  2  1

# Contents

# Foreword

Those who occupy positions of leadership, or are destined to do so, or who simply are intrigued by the exercise of leadership, will find *The Entrepreneurial President* a most welcome addition. James L. Fisher and James V. Koch, both former college presidents and consultants to governing boards and presidents, have generated the largest empirical study yet of presidential attitudes, values, and behavior. The duo, who previously limned the theory and practicalities of presidential leadership in Presidential Leadership (1996), now present us with a wealth of detail about the beliefs and values of twenty-first-century presidents. Even more important, they supply us with fascinating, unprecedented data concerning the ways college presidents actually do lead and how the views and behavior of successful presidents differ from those whose careers are more pedestrian.

The nature of the American college presidency has changed substantially in recent years. Relative to the mid-1980s, when Fisher, Tack, and Wheeler (1988) performed the first statistically rigorous empirical study of presidential attitudes and values, the roster of college presidents today is considerably more diverse. Far more women and members of minority groups now lead our colleges, and the activities and focal points of all presidents steadily have become more external to their campuses. Today's college presidents are expected to be masters of sensitive external relationships involving groups as disparate as adversarial neighborhood civic leagues and the National Science Foundation, and to converse knowledgeably with individuals ranging from economic development officials to U.S. senators. The contemporary college presidency demands versatile individuals who are indefatigable, prolific fund-raisers; who can speak fluently to the local Rotary or to a group of venture capitalists; and who understand and are able to capitalize upon the peculiar, larger-than-life role that intercollegiate athletics play in our society. Yes, college presidents must still be academic leaders. However, as Fisher and Koch show, they now allocate a majority of their time to these and similar external issues and challenges and perhaps exemplify the "Captains of Erudition" whom Thorstein Veblen (1918) critiqued.

Fisher and Koch present persuasive data demonstrating that the most effective and successful college presidents today are entrepreneurial in outlook and behavior. They are intelligent risk takers who are not afraid to disturb the status quo. They prize innovation and value differing points of view. Synergistic alliances with business and governmental agencies are second nature to them. They use, but do not overuse, technology as a part of their leadership styles. Fisher and Koch's groundbreaking data reveal that women presidents tend to be more entrepreneurial than men presidents. This finding alone will make their work a seminal contribution.

If you wish to know what college presidents actually think and how they actually behave, this is the book for you. It is must reading for all who are interested in the American college presidency and leadership in general.

*Gene A. Budig*

# Preface

In 1988, James L. Fisher, Martha W. Tack, and Karen J. Wheeler published the first large-sample, statistically rigorous, replicable empirical study of the attitudes and values of American college presidents. This study provided groundbreaking data about presidents. In *The Entrepreneurial President*, we update Fisher, Tack, and Wheeler and extend their work in several critical ways. First, we place considerable focus on actual presidential behavior in addition to attitudes and values. Second, we include much larger samples of women and minority presidents, whose numbers have increased tremendously in the past 15 years. We explicitly compare women and minority presidents to men presidents and Caucasian presidents. Third, we include numerous control variables that reflect the character of the president's institution. Fourth, we focus substantially on the entrepreneurial attitudes and behavior of presidents and how these things determine presidential success. Fifth, we examine the extent to which presidential academic training and reliance upon technology affect presidential success. Sixth, we introduce a multivariate model that permits us to examine how a variety of factors related to presidential success influence each other and presidential behavior.

Our results are thought provoking and may be controversial in some quarters because they challenge some established views of the world. We invite others to follow in our footsteps and extend our knowledge of leadership in general and American college presidents in particular. The pursuit of truth is a never-ending process.

We owe special thanks to P. Neal Meier and Carl Schramm for their support and encouragement for this project, to the Kauffman Foundation for its generous financial support, to Professor Reginald Worthley for his expert statistical advice, to Xi Wu for her extremely productive research assistance, and to our wives, Kimberly Fisher and Donna Koch, for their many years of patient, encouraging, didactic support for us and our work.

# CHAPTER 1

## The Notion of the Entrepreneurial Leader

The nation felt another leadership, nervous, aggressive, and strong.
—Margaret Leech, describing Theodore Roosevelt,
*In the Days of McKinley*, 1959

In all human affairs, the odds are always six to five against.
—Damon Runyon, journalist and raconteur

Without risks, we're all caretakers.
—Leonard Stern, corporate CEO

### THE ENTREPRENEURIAL LEADER

There are few notions in modern America discussed and dissected more than the notion of leadership. The thoughts and actions of individuals ranging from Jesus Christ and Attila the Hun to Abraham Lincoln and Colin Powell have become fodder for discussions of leadership and leaders. In April 2003, we performed an Internet book search for the term *leadership* at the Barnes & Noble.com Web site and found an astonishing 13,433 entries. By any standard, that's a lot of writing. Yet, the number of books relating to *entrepreneurship* was hardly modest, either—1,998 entries at Barnes & Noble.com.

Even so, as we shall see, relatively few studies have visibly connected leadership and leaders to entrepreneurial attitudes and activity. Our hypothesis is that common ground exists between the classic and tested characteristics of the leader and those of the entrepreneur. Indeed, the most successful leaders frequently are entrepreneurial in attitudes and behavior, and we introduce strong empirical evidence to this effect. This evidence relates to college presidents[1] and is based upon an exceedingly large and detailed sample (N = 713) of such individuals. Effective, successful college presidents today are bold, change-oriented leaders who appreciate, but are not anchored by, the past and who readily question the status quo, generate innovative ideas, and find ways to prevent organizational structure from discouraging change. In a phrase, they are transformational leaders who make a difference.

## THE NOTION OF THE ENTREPRENEURIAL LEADER

Do entrepreneurial leaders really exist in today's American colleges and universities? Do college presidents often behave in an entrepreneurial fashion, and does this behavior pay off for them and their institutions? Are some presidents more likely to exhibit entrepreneurial attitudes than others? The answers to these and similar questions are the subject of this book. However, the answers depend substantially upon what one means by *entrepreneurial*.

*Entrepreneur* is derived from an old French verb, *entreprendre*, meaning "to undertake." The *Encarta World English Dictionary* (1999, 597) defines an entrepreneur as "somebody who sets up and finances new commercial enterprises to make a profit," while the *Merriam-Webster Unabridged Dictionary, Electronic Version* (2003) says an entrepreneur is "one who organizes, manages, and assumes the risks of a business or enterprise." Interestingly, *The Oxford English Dictionary's* (2003) first definition of an entrepreneur is one who is "the director or manager of a public musical institution," but it notes that in the area of political economy, an entrepreneur is "one who undertakes an enterprise; one who owns and manages a business; a person who takes the risk of profit or loss." *Oxford* further notes that the first known English usage of the word was in 1852 by Thomas Carlyle, who spoke of gambling houses constructed by a "French gambling entrepreneur." This somewhat unsavory connotation has colored the use of the word entrepreneur throughout the twentieth century and has made the label *entrepreneurial college president* a mixed compliment in some higher education circles.

If one accepts the original sense of the French verb *entreprendre*, "to undertake," then virtually every college president is entrepreneurial because all are involved on a daily basis in numerous undertakings. Taking this view, nearly every individual, college president or not, without exception would qualify as an entrepreneur. If, however, one prefers the *Encarta* definition that an entrepreneur is one who is engaged in activity designed to generate a profit, then most college presidents are entrepreneurs to a much more limited extent. While most campuses support some activities (bookstores, food services, intercollegiate athletics) that could generate profits, the bulk of conventional campus activity is not directly designed to generate profits, and only a few academic institutions find themselves even capable statistically of making such calculations.

Many frown on overt profit- and revenue-oriented behavior by college presidents. Edmund Burke's eighteenth-century lament that, "The age of chivalry is gone. That of sophisters, economists and calculators has succeeded" (1909), continues to fall on sympathetic ears in much of academe. Prestigious contemporary observers such as former Harvard President Derek Bok (2003a,b) have issued warnings to presidents and governing boards about putting the university and its values on sale, though Harvard itself has become heavily involved in a variety of commercial endeavors.

Nonetheless, in recent years, traditional views of academe have been challenged by the rise of a burgeoning for-profit sector of higher education. Firms such as the Apollo Group, DeVry, Sylvan, and Phoenix have gained significant market shares in higher education and all are publicly traded firms listed on either the New York Stock Exchange or NASDAQ. The University of Phoenix has become the largest private university in the United States, while DeVry Institute campuses exist in most major metropolitan areas.

A common presumption is that the increased focus of nonprofit colleges and universities on profit-generating, or at least revenue-generating activities, plus the emergence of the for-profit institutions, have altered the role of the college president. One might reasonably postulate that the allocation of presidential time has changed because there is increased emphasis upon revenue-generating activities. Further, one might hypothesize that the training and previous experience of college presidents have evolved to include entrepreneurial activities. Admittedly, these are reasonable extrapolations. But we must be careful here. First, there is a paucity of evidence on these issues. We don't really know how businesslike or entrepreneurial the typical college president is (or is not). None of the previous studies of college presidents has focused upon entrepreneurial issues.

Second, we know remarkably little about the presidents of for-profit campuses. Traditionally, they either have been ignored as irrelevant or deemed by some to be less worthy because of their focus on filthy lucre. For many, for-profit institutions and their presidents have constituted a shadowy, even dark corner of higher education. Thus, based upon the evidence available, it is impossible to say how, if at all, these presidents differ from their not-for-profit brethren.

Third, "separation of ownership and management" (Berle and Means, 1932) typically exists on nearly all campuses, but especially on for-profit campuses. The owners of for-profit colleges and universities are relatively easy to identify; they are the stockholders. It is less clear who owns the far more numerous not-for-profit institutions. Governing boards function as the proxies for taxpayer owners in public institutions and serve as the legal corpora of independent institutions. In either case, however, the governing boards seldom actually manage the institutions they putatively own. That is, the governing boards do not also function as the campus presidents, except in a very few cases involving very small, for-profit institutions.

Thus, there is separation of ownership and management in American higher education, and only rarely do the presidents of colleges and universities, even those that are for-profit, have any ownership in those institutions. In that respect, they do not differ significantly from corporate and business sector chief executives, who despite recent trends to reward them with company stock, usually do not own significant portions of their firms. The upshot of this separation of ownership and management in colleges and universities is this: governing boards and college presidents may have divergent interests. This implies that governing boards may find it difficult to persuade or even to force college presidents to implement policies the presidents do not like. Presidential independence of action may exist more often than casual observers believe. On occasion, this may reflect a position of great strength that has been carved out by many years of hard-driving, successful presidential performance (John Silber and William Harvey come to mind). Alternatively, it may reflect a lack of knowledge by the governing board of campus affairs, sometimes brought about deliberately by a president who hides many actions from the view of the board. Or, regardless of rhetoric, it could reflect disinterest by governing boards.

The *Merriam-Webster* and *Oxford* definitions of the word *entrepreneur* place emphasis upon entrepreneurial risk taking. Entrepreneurs, then, are individuals who undertake activities involving risk and uncertainty, terms that many individuals use interchangeably.[2] It is this view of entrepreneurial activity that predominates today when one talks about entrepreneurial college presidents. Botstein (1985), for example, urges that presidents become "consummate risk takers" (124) who marshal their own talents and those of others to achieve valuable ends. Profit and loss considerations are not necessarily involved, though they may be. Regardless, the emphasis is upon the individual college president making decisions that entail risks to her own institution and perhaps to herself as well. Consider some examples.

> If one raises admissions standards, enrollment may decline (or it may rise). There is uncertainty involved.
>
> If one initiates a distance-learning program, the institution may lose money, and hostile faculty may pose critical academic questions. Alternatively, the institution may tap hitherto unreachable populations and prosper, generating an era of good feelings on campus. However, by no means is the outcome certain.
>
> If one decides to move the institution's intercollegiate athletic programs from, say, the NCAA's Division II to its Division I, then its teams might have trouble competing and lose more games. Consequently, fan interest might dwindle and financial losses could result. Or, instead, the institution might acquire public support, win championships, and make money. Which will occur on the campus of Ole Siwash?
>
> If a president decides to outsource his institution's residence halls, then students might be displeased with the result and decide to live on their own, off-campus. On the other hand, students may fall in love with the new model and make the residence halls the place to be. Presidents who have made the wrong decision in this situation have lost their jobs.

An endless number of additional examples could be produced. The point is that any college president who has a heartbeat is likely to take risks as she performs her job. These may be minimal in nature (privatizing the campus bookstore), or they may be substantial and gamble with the institution's future (Muskingum College lowering tuition in a time of substantial tuition increases). In either case, there are alternatives and there are consequences, though neither may be known perfectly. Those who succeed in this milieu may be wise, lucky, or both.

The eminent economic historian Joseph Schumpeter (1923), who coined the oft-cited phrase, "perennial waves of creative destruction," to describe the dynamic processes of entrepreneurial capitalism, opined that "the defining characteristic [of an entrepreneur] is simply the doing of new things or the doing of things that are already being done in a different way" (89). In Schumpeter's view, innovations occur (and old ways die) because some have the courage to do things differently, to take risks, and to place themselves and their institutions on the line.

Attached to nearly any substantive decision is a set of choices, each of which involves potential risks (but also rewards). All presidents engage in risk-taking behavior on a daily basis. Yet some apparently take more and bigger risks than others. Some apparently risk (gamble?) their institution's future (and their own) by adopting courses of action for which the final outcome is not clear. Further, some presidents swim upstream against prevailing currents and advice when they do so. Needless to say, some lose their jobs as a consequence, though presidential sackings seem most often to relate to interpersonal problems and the inability of the incumbent to get along with key groups such as members of the governing board or faculty.

## THE FOCUS OF THE WORK REPORTED HERE

The empirical work reported in this study was supported by a generous grant from the Kauffman Foundation, which historically has exhibited great interest in the study of entrepreneurial activity.

Among the questions we attempt to answer in this study are:

How entrepreneurial are college presidents?

What are their attitudes toward entrepreneurial activities and risk taking?

Do entrepreneurial presidents have different work habits?

How is perceived presidential success related to entrepreneurial attitudes and activities?

Do the institutions of entrepreneurial presidents grow more, receive more gifts, attract better students, or have better reputations than presidents who are less entrepreneurial?

Are entrepreneurial presidents regarded with disdain by other presidents?

Are there gender differences in presidential entrepreneurial views and activities?

Are there ethnic differences?

Are there age differences?

Does experience influence presidential entrepreneurial attitudes and activities?

Does presidential experience make a difference?

Does experience outside higher education make a difference?

Does the nature of previous academic positions held influence entrepreneurial attitudes and activities?

Does previous academic training in areas such as accounting, computer science, and economics make a difference?

Are there differences in entrepreneurial attitudes and activities between the presidents of public and independent institutions?

Two-year versus four-year institutions?

Liberal arts colleges versus comprehensive institutions versus research institutions?

Are some regions of the country more fertile grounds for entrepreneurial attitudes and activities than others?

## HOW WILL WE ANSWER THESE QUESTIONS?

While we clearly could supply our own hunches to answer the previous questions or engage in a more sophisticated a priori analysis that would lead to predicted answers, our approach in this book is to provide the reader with a substantial amount of empirical evidence about institutions, their presidents, and presidential attitudes, values, and behavior. During 2002, we received, recorded, and analyzed highly detailed surveys sent to us by more than 700 college and university presidents. The data generated by these surveys provide an unprecedented look at college presidents and their attitudes, values, and behavior. This is the largest such sample ever drawn from the *entire* universe of American college presidents. The sample spans all of higher education—public and independent institutions, religious and secular institutions, institutions with and without collective bargaining, institutions within all nine of the Carnegie Commission institutional categories, not-for-profit and for-profit institutions, colleges, and universities located in all regions of the United States. It differs from the well-regarded biannual survey of presidents conducted by the American Council on Education (2002) in that it focuses primarily on presidential attitudes, values, and behavior rather than on describing them demographically. We are interested in the demographics of American college presidents, but only as they might influence presidential thoughts and actions.

We divide the 713 presidents in our sample into two groups—371 presidents designated by an expert as being "effective" and the remainder (342 presidents in number), whom we deem "representative." We then compare and contrast the two groups using rigorous statistical methods, including multivariate analysis. The fundamental question is this—Are the effective presidents different from the representative presidents? If so, how? And, of course, we are especially interested in whether college presidents as a group exhibit entrepreneurial attitudes and behavior. Does the vessel that some label "the entrepreneurial president" ultimately contain any water? By focusing on survey responses that appear to relate to entrepreneurial attitudes and behavior, we examine whether the effective presidents are more or less entrepreneurial than the representative presidents.

## OUR PLAN FOR THE REMAINDER OF THE BOOK

Six chapters follow. In chapter 2, we review relevant literature with respect to entrepreneurialism in higher education and entrepreneurial college and university presidents. Chapter 3 describes in detail the process by which we obtained our survey data and the survey instrument itself. Chapter 4 presents a series of statistical tests that focus on any differences that may exist between effective and representative presidents. Chapters 5 and 6 are devoted to additional statistical analysis of the survey results. Chapter 5 focuses on differences between women and men presidents and minority and Caucasian presidents, while our analysis in chapter 6 concentrates upon hypotheses relating to entrepreneurial presidential attitudes, values, and behavior and their ramifications for presidential behavior. In chapter 7, we refute the notion that the age of transformational, presidential "titans" is over and present the reader with profiles of several presidents who clearly exhibit entrepreneurial behavior and have transformed their institutions.

# CHAPTER

# A Review of Relevant Work

The first task of a leader is to define reality.
—Max DePree, former CEO of Herman Miller in
*Leadership Is an Art* (1989)

There's still a requirement for leaders to take educated risks.
—Jeffrey Garten, dean of the Yale Business School, in
*Business Week*, 17 February 2003

I see it said that leaders should keep their ears to the ground. All I can say is that the British nation will find it very hard to look up to the leaders who are detected in that somewhat ungainly posture.
—Sir Winston Churchill

## ENTREPRENEURSHIP AND HIGHER EDUCATION: SELDOM HAVE THE TWAIN MET

While the concept of an entrepreneur is part of an old and honored tradition in areas such as economics and business, the application of this image to higher education, and especially to college presidents, is a relatively recent phenomenon. The Carnegie Council's 1980 final report, *Three Thousand Futures: The Next Twenty Years for Higher Education*, contains more than 400 subject index entries concerning the status and future of higher education, but nary a mention of entrepreneurs, entrepreneurial attitudes, or entrepreneurial college presidents. Mayhew's (1979) oft-cited

*Surviving the Eighties* similarly did not treat these matters, nor did Levine's extensive 1993 volume, *Higher Learning in America, 1980–2000.*

Nor have otherwise voluble college presidents spent much time talking about the entrepreneurial nature (or lack thereof) of their activities. The view of a national figure such as Clark Kerr (1972, 1984) of the University of California is representative; despite believing that presidents make a difference, he often chose to emphasize the role of the college president as a mediator among competing interests, on- and off-campus, rather than as an entrepreneur. Or consider an innovative though ultimately unsuccessful president such as Richard Berendzen (1986) of American University, who chose to emphasize the undeniable social and political whirl of the presidency in the nation's capital rather than entrepreneurial topics. More recently, Syracuse University's estimable Kenneth "Buzz" Shaw (1999) wrote appealingly of "Buzz Words on Leadership," but entrepreneurialism was not among them. Or contemplate the sage observations of Gene Budig, who achieved fame both as a university president and as the president of the American League. He aptly described the college presidency as involving *A Game of Uncommon Skill* (2002), but once again he did not choose to focus on the entrepreneurial tendencies of the activities of presidents.

Even those writers who appear to have entrepreneurial college presidencies in mind ordinarily do not speak of them in those terms. Fisher, Tack, and Wheeler (1988), in their landmark empirical study of effective college presidents, wrote of "bold" decision makers, "risk takers," "innovation," and "aggressive opportunism," but did not explicitly mention entrepreneurs or entrepreneurial activities. Similarly, Bass's (1990) catholic survey of leadership theory and research contains numerous references to entrepreneurial leaders, but none that applies explicitly to higher education. Bass does not explicitly define entrepreneurial activity, but he typically equates it with risk taking by a leader, though at other times he uses the term almost synonymously with innovation. In the literature concerning primarily nonacademic management and leadership, the term *entrepreneur* is used with frequency. For example, in a well-known article, Mintzberg (1975) categorized *entrepreneur* as one of six roles a manager might fulfill.

## PECK'S GROUNDBREAKING ANALYSIS

Some writers, usually not college presidents, have explicitly considered the entrepreneurial attitudes and activities of college presidents. One of the first to do so extensively was Peck (1983), who talked of "The Entrepreneurial College Presidency" in his examination of 19 small, independent colleges who, he argued, had successful, entrepreneurial presidents. Peck found these successful presidents to be "future focused" and forthrightly stated that "The small independent college is an entrepreneurial enterprise and its leaders are entrepreneurs in the best classical sense" (20). He argued that "the concept of entrepreneurship . . . is required to comprehend the development of the American education system" (20). Given that Peck's work on entrepreneurial presidents was the first substantive work to appear in the area, it is worth our time to hone in on his arguments. Even though Peck presented only anecdotal evidence and his work is not scientifically replicable, he is an extremely fruitful source of the hypotheses we will test empirically.

Peck cautioned that it would be incorrect to conclude that all education endeavors are entrepreneurial. He also noted that many colleges and universities that are entrepreneurial in an overall sense have many divisions and departments that are not entrepreneurial in character. That is, matters entrepreneurial and entrepreneurs themselves often are found only in certain parts of an institution—those that in Peck's words are "future focused" rather than concentrating upon day-to-day operations. Frequently, one of those sites is the president's office.

Further, he postulated that academic entrepreneurs shine most when confronting "ambiguity, confusion and unpredictability" (20). This notion is borrowed from Cohen and March (1974 and 1986) who, in contrast to Peck, concluded that the typical president ultimately was rather powerless to do anything about such conditions. However, the successful college presidents in Peck's sample thrived on uncertainty and actually capitalized on it by sorting the wheat from the chaff and then moving ahead boldly in circumstances that seemingly paralyzed less-successful presidents. Many entrepreneurial presidents, then, were individuals who thrived in bad times, perhaps because the times appeared to require decisive, innovative action. They were in the mold of Franklin Delano Roosevelt, not Warren Harding.

How and when do entrepreneurial college presidents appear? According to Peck,

> Entrepreneurship usually appears when there is no precedent. For the problem, when it cannot be understood, *ex ante*; when the entire course of events cannot be specified; or when there is a high level of ambiguity; or when an unprecedented unanticipated change of circumstances calls for a change in priorities or an altogether new approach; or when actions depend—to a significant degree—on the skills, temperament, attitudes, and commitments of persons associated with the institution (20).

Peck also believed he observed the tendency for successful, entrepreneurial presidents to make decisions based substantially upon their own intuition. He underlined that this intuitive approach to decision making was not irrational and presumed previous hard work, data gathering, and analysis. In Peck's eyes, intuitive decision making was a creative response to challenging circumstances and necessarily involved a high degree of risk.

Peck's successful presidents were, in his view, people-oriented persons who "administered through people, not structures" (21). This frequently involved many face-to-face meetings. Crises were handled directly and often without regard to the college's formal organization as the institution's president would deal directly with the individuals involved, regardless of the chain of command.

The successful, entrepreneurial presidents, Peck said, "appear not to control or manage but to supervise...they are brokers of change, interpreters of policy...." (21). That is, his entrepreneurial presidents were deeply immersed in their institutions but were not micromanagers. Instead, they saw the larger picture and were skilled at perceiving trends.

But Peck's entrepreneurial presidents were not addicted to strategic planning, which he believes suppresses innovation. "There is no place in such systems for intuition, innovation or opportunism...." (21). He argued further that institutions that adopt plans and attempt to live by those plans have "effectively blocked the freedom essential for innovation, change, adaptation and formative reaction" (21). Of course, plans can be changed. Nonetheless, to change the plan repeatedly is to abandon it. That is why Peck found that more than a few of his presidents lost interest in comprehensive institutional planning. But the act of planning can be useful, and Peck allows that planning is a means by which members of the institution's varied constituencies communicate with each other, even if the end result does not turn out to be useful.

Peck's entrepreneurial presidents worked through their colleagues, but "the colleges that were investigated are not run by committees, nor are they driven by master plans" (22). These successful presidents exercised strong and assertive leadership, but they did so in the context by relying upon, and collaborating with, their colleagues. These presidents appear to have honored the letter and spirit of the *1966 Joint Statement on Governance*, which is the most accepted statement of the meaning of shared governance in academe.

Among the means by which Peck's entrepreneurial presidents acquired information were to walk the campus, attend many campus events, network with key colleagues, attend service club meetings in the community, and read voluminous materials. This intelligence gathering served as a source of, and a testing ground for, new ideas. As such, it was the basis for many of the entrepreneurial activities of the presidents, who liberally borrowed from each other.

Effective, entrepreneurial presidents in Peck's world were future oriented, but they resisted tying themselves into long-term commitments. They thought about the future and acted upon it, but they preferred to identify and keep open alternate courses of action.

Finally, what were the demographic characteristics of Peck's entrepreneurial presidents? The typical entrepreneurial president was a man who possessed a baccalaureate degree from a similar institution and a terminal degree from a large public institution. He/she had experience as a faculty member in an area other than business or a career-oriented discipline. Although Peck says, "there is no obvious connection between scholarly work and the administration of a college" (24), scholarly activity is important because it demonstrates understanding and commitment to the institution's raison d'être.

Peck concluded with a central question: Where do the characteristics of the entrepreneurial president come from? What is the source of the president's courage to take risks, ability to change and adapt, and propensity to innovate? "Only further investigations will tell," he wryly observed (25). Peck's inability to say more is, in fact, one of the motivating reasons for this study. Do entrepreneurial presidents have common backgrounds, experiences, education, and learning patterns that contribute to their entrepreneurial behavior? Or, as some argue, are these things almost genetic and not conducive to learning? We provide evidence on these and many other related issues.

## THE KAUFFMAN FOUNDATION'S IMPETUS

The Kauffman Foundation founded and supports the Center for Entrepreneurial Leadership Clearing House on Entrepreneurial Education (CELCEE), which is a rich source of information for anyone interested in either entrepreneurs or entrepreneurial behavior. The center has examined certain aspects of entrepreneurial activity in North American colleges and universities. Its focus is threefold. First, it examines for-profit research commercialization and technology transfer. Second, it traces performance contracting by institutions where, for example, the institutions contract to educate specific individuals for specific labor-market slots in areas such as information technology. Third, to a lesser extent, it has focused on the state of entrepreneurial education in colleges and universities. Presidents appear in the center's work only incidentally, although it is apparent that college presidents must set the agenda for change.

The Kauffman Foundation has given less attention to noncommercial entrepreneurial activity within colleges and universities. However, as Balderston (1995) has pointed out, "the pulses of academic change" (91) are fertile areas for entrepreneurial activity. Curricular reform provides an example, though Balderston notes that truly entrepreneurial changes in curricula tend to be "episodic" (91).

Other opportunities for innovation and entrepreneurial approaches to the affairs of higher education exist with respect to how faculty are recruited, appointed, and evaluated, how faculty time is allocated, and how faculty are rewarded. An illustration is the notion that an increasing proportion of faculty evaluation should focus on academic departments rather than upon the individuals. Similarly, there is considerable room for entrepreneurial approaches to distance learning and the introduction of information technology into courses. One might also focus on implementing entrepreneurial approaches to restructuring the administrative organization and reporting lines, developing innovative ways to advise and place students, mounting inventive ways to recruit students by utilizing alumni, and executing novel approaches to raising funds. Thus, there are numerous areas of a modern college or university that can, and do, involve entrepreneurial instincts and approaches.

The entrepreneurial focus of the Kauffman Foundation underlines a dichotomy that typically exists in discussions of collegiate entrepreneurial leadership and activities. Most attention has been given to ostensibly revenue-producing entrepreneurial ventures, for example, the commercialization of research and development activities, or the development of executive education programs and branch campuses. Less attention has been devoted to collegiate activities that may not have direct revenue-producing potential. However, as we have just noted, entrepreneurial college presidents need not overtly pursue revenue or profit in order to go about their work in an innovative or path-breaking fashion. "Stacking the academic dominoes in a different fashion" (the words of one of the author's mentors) may not merit mention in the *Wall Street Journal*. Nonetheless, such activity may bring to the fore a leader's invaluable ability to stand above the fray and look at a situation from a new and fresh perspective. Like an innovative musical composer who develops an important new musical genre, an accomplished and skillful academic entrepreneur views the world though a different lens, comprehends relationships that others have overlooked, and (most importantly) finds the ways and means to bring this distinctive vision to reality.

Our consideration of entrepreneurialism in higher education will rely upon a more inclusive notion of entrepreneurial activity—one that is inclusive of both profit-oriented and nonprofit-oriented entrepreneurial efforts. In our view, entrepreneurs exist in all segments of American society, not only those that pursue the profit motive. Hence, there can be (and are) entrepreneurial clergy, kindergarten teachers, military officers, social workers and, yes, college presidents—whether or not they act in direct response to a profit-and-loss statement.

## AGNOSTICS, CRITICS, AND UNBELIEVERS

There has been little consideration of the role or potential of entrepreneurial leadership in higher education. Why so? First and foremost, some seasoned observers of the American college presidency believe that relatively few presidents ever make a noticeable difference in their institutions, much less engage in visibly entrepreneurial activity. Cohen and March (1974, 1986), in a frequently cited study based primarily upon their analysis of 31 presidents, asserted that "the president's role [is] more commonly sporadic and symbolic than significant" (1986, 2). March (1980, 21) famously suggested that presidents are interchangeable like lightbulbs, and "It is hard to tell the difference between two different light bulbs." Though Cohen and March in their later edition softened their stance slightly on whether college presidents could truly make a difference, they nonetheless opined (1986, 203) that "It is probably a mistake for a college president to imagine that what he does in office affects significantly either the long-run position of the institution or his reputation as a president." The Cohen and March duo discounts the possibility that individual presidents leave their imprint on their institutions. "Colleges make presidents, not the reverse," they argue (79). They see the president's role as "more commonly sporadic and symbolic than significant" because presidents operate on campuses characterized by "organized anarchy" such that many different constituencies can and do make decisions autonomously (2).

Rather than the institution becoming Emerson's "lengthened shadow of a great man" (Atkinson, 1940), Cohen and March see most presidents disappearing into the shadows or the penumbra of the institution such that they ultimately affect its path only marginally. The presidents that Cohen and March see are not entrepreneurs, but pedestrian managers, vote takers and bureaucrats, even if they see themselves otherwise. Botstein (1985, 105) in a well-known essay, seconded this motion by concluding that "the position of president has come to be viewed as a singularly unenviable—even a beleaguered and impossible—one." He added that, "the college president has not only become quite marginal in intellectual terms but possesses little real power" (106). This is an ironic observation, coming from an indi-

vidual who is widely conceded to have been an influential and transformational president in his own right at several institutions, most recently
at Bard College. Fortunately, Botstein concludes that his generalization
does not constitute the inescapable fate of college presidents, and suggests
how they might avoid such ignominy.

In this view, colleges and universities are intensely bureaucratic institutions that resist change and, perforce, parry or frustrate most presidential entrepreneurial initiatives of any consequence. This might describe
many large and complex organizations, but it seems to have particular rel-
evance for higher education, where inertia and process often reign supreme.
Witness Weinstein's *Moving a Battleship with Your Bare Hands* (1993). Getz,
Siegfried, and Anderson (1997), in a landmark study of the adoption of 30
of the most important innovations in higher education, found that on average, 26 years were required for the median institution to adopt a typical
innovation such as an automated library circulation system. This is not
lightning progress.

Higher education seldom moves rapidly toward any objective. Just as
President John F. Kennedy bemoaned the unresponsiveness of the federal
bureaucracy to his blandishments in the early 1960s, many a college president has found that she cannot easily move her institution from its established ruts. The maritime metaphor about a college being like a huge ocean
liner that can come about and change its direction only very slowly continues to be apt.

## TRANSFORMATIONAL VERSUS TRANSACTIONAL LEADERSHIP

In recent years, many writers have differentiated between *transactional*
and *transformational* leadership (Burns, 1978). At the extreme, transactional leaders are vote takers who simply reflect the majority will of the
individuals with whom they deal. More often, they are individuals who in
the words of Birnbaum (1988) are "engaged in...transactions with the
environment and with internal subsystems in an effort to detect problems
and to make the adjustments necessary to keep the institution in harmony
with its environment" (204). These are leaders who strive to avoid crises
and make midcourse adjustments but do not impose grand personal visions
on their institutions. Cohen and March (1986), for example, see American college presidents as individuals who react rather than initiate and
whose time is "largely controlled by the desires of others" (1).

Why do college presidents behave in this fashion? An important reason, say Cohen and March (1986), is the very nature of American colleges

and universities. They argue that the typical American college or university "does not know what it is doing. Its goals are either vague or in dispute...its major participants wander in and out of the organization.... These factors do not make a university a bad organization or a disorganized one; but they do make it a problem to describe, understand, and lead" (3). Thus, Cohen and March believe even determined presidents find they cannot really make a significant institutional imprint and end up behaving in a transactional mode.

Transformational leaders, on the other hand, are individuals who possess a strong and captivating vision that they rely upon to motivate and change their institutions. They possess "visionary intelligence," according to Gilley, Fulmer, and Reithlingshoefer (1986).

Transformational leaders also recognize and become expert in utilizing the elements of power (French and Raven, 1959; Fisher, 1984) in order to affect change. They rely upon coercive, reward, legitimate, expert, and charismatic sources of power in order to convince individuals to undertake tasks and do things that these individuals otherwise would ignore or reject (Dahl, 1957). Wright (1988) has expressed this aspect of the transformational presidency succinctly: "The exercise of power is an essential element of effective leadership" (88).

Of course, power can be used for good or ill. However, in the eyes of Burns (1978, 2003) and Fisher (1984), effective, transformational leaders do not regard the use of power to achieve their vision as an ominous vice, and they do not use power for inappropriate personal aggrandizement. Instead, they understand that unless one is exceedingly lucky, few good things occur in the long run without the application and exercise of power. To some presidents, the use of power seems almost inborn, and they gracefully and skillfully utilize the sources of power to achieve their worthy goals. Some college presidents seem to manipulate the levers of power almost unconsciously. They are those naturally gifted individuals who are able to convince other individuals to adopt their vision as their own and pursue it enthusiastically. For other presidents, however, the ability to understand and exercise power does not come easily and must be studied, acquired, and honed. Unfortunately, as Fisher and Koch (1996) point out, many individuals are uncomfortable discussing the sources of power and its utilization. In some academic quarters, Lord Acton's oft-quoted proviso that "power corrupts" is taken as inerrant gospel. Fisher and Koch, relying upon Kipnis (1976), comment, "Many people think acts of power are engaged in by dark and pernicious figures unlike anyone they know, least of all themselves" (10). Nevertheless, the exercise of power is essential to any transformational college presidency. Transformational presidents, nearly all of whom are entrepreneurial, use power in order to take the intelligent, calculated risks that enable them to transform their institutions and make them superior places to be.

But some observers believe that transformational behavior can be counterproductive, or even destructive (Walker, 1979; Sellers, 2002; Useem, 2002; Burns, 2003). A contemporary disciple of Cohen and March is Birnbaum (1988, 1992, 2000), who stresses how institutions of higher education are resistant to change. He writes knowledgeably about colleges, presidents, governing boards, and the management fads that plague institutions of higher education. Birnbaum ultimately concludes that "attempts at transformational leadership are more likely to lead to disruption and conflict than to desirable outcomes" (1992, 29). He also contends that campuses tend to revert to their former circumstances when supposedly transformational presidents depart. Ultimately, he argues, "Most presidents have short-term, marginal, positive, instrumental effects on their colleagues; these effects would likely not be different under another president with similar qualifications" (169). Hence, Birnbaum's presidential lightbulbs are somewhat less interchangeable than those of March, but only to a degree. In the Birnbaumian world, most appropriately qualified and experienced presidents cannot be differentiated from each other in the long run, and they ultimately have the same impact.

The prospect that some transformational leaders eventually run their institutions into the proverbial ditch has been noted and feared by many individuals. The reasons for this are several. Sometimes the risk-taking entrepreneur does not undertake appropriate due diligence of alternatives and thereafter takes unwise risks. Or, after a visible stream of successes, some leaders begin to believe they are infallible and have so much faith in themselves that they believe they cannot fail. Whether Adolf Hitler or 1990s corporate leader Al "Chainsaw" Dunlap, they often find out differently. And, after a period of time, it sometimes becomes clear that the audacious goals of some transformational leaders are shabby, immoral, or even illegal (Burns, 2003). Thus, some organizations eschew the opportunity to appoint transformational leaders and instead opt for CEOs who are "disciplined, deferential, and even a bit dull" (Sellers, 66).

## EMPIRICAL STUDIES

The only previous statistically rigorous, replicable, large-sample study of American college presidential effectiveness at all institutional levels was that undertaken by Fisher, Tack, and Wheeler (1988). This study, when it appeared, filled a noticeable void that had caused Vroom (1983, 367), in a review of leadership research in higher education, to comment that "remarkably little research has been conducted on institutions of higher education" relative to questions of leadership. This was especially true with respect to empirical studies.

Fisher, Tack, and Wheeler found that presidents perceived to be effective (those who were transformational) were distinctive in attitudes and operation. In short, they differed from other presidents. Fisher, Tack, and Wheeler reported that effective transformational leaders typically were charismatic, were older and more experienced than the average president, held impressive academic pedigrees and had significant refereed publications, were not afraid to challenge the status quo, believed in merit pay, maintained some degree of social distance from their colleagues, welcomed innovation, supported and cultivated unconventional people, were themselves innovative, exuded energy and confidence, and were somewhat less collegial than other presidents but were warm and friendly.

Fisher, Tack, and Wheeler's effective college presidents were much more likely to agree with the statement "The effective leader takes risks" than were other presidents (69). To wit, presidents who were nominated at least twice by experts as being especially effective were considerably more likely to agree with this statement ($p < .04$ using a chi-square test). Fisher and Tack (1988) later had more to say about this in a collection of essays written by and about college presidents. There, they did not mince words: "Thus, the president must be a risk taker, one who studies the situation carefully (but not too long to lose the opportunity) and takes decisive action" (2).

While the words *transformational* and *entrepreneurial* are not synonymous, it is almost impossible for a college president to become transformational and to change the path of her institution without her also being entrepreneurial and taking intelligent, shrewdly calculated risks. Indeed, while Fisher, Tack, and Wheeler (1988) did not talk about entrepreneurial college presidents as such, it seems apparent they had these individuals in mind when they divided their sample of presidents into those who were effective and the remainder who were representative. The Fisher-Tack-Wheeler effective presidents often were "innovative," "bold," and "opportunity conscious"; they exercised "creativity," exhibited "imagination," engaged in "risk taking," and evinced "aggressive opportunism" (chapter 2). They concluded that "researchers use the terms transforming, transformational, and innovative interchangeably" (23). We will not add *entrepreneurial* to that list here, but we emphasize that entrepreneurial presidents are quite likely to be transformational, and vice versa.

Another empirical study of note involved 718 junior and community college presidents. McFarlin, Crittenden, and Ebbers (1999) put their research question this way: "Are there systematic differences between the backgrounds of 'powerful, effective, and inspirational leaders' versus the backgrounds of 'ambivalent, risk-averting individuals?'" Accordingly, they identified 96 "outstanding" presidents in their sample, with the remaining 622 being "normative." As did Fisher, Tack, and Wheeler, they found the outstanding presidents to have more presidential experience than the ordinary, normative presidents and to be slightly older, but also to have been younger when they assumed their first presidency. Their outstanding junior and community college presidents also were more heavily male and more often married than the normative group, and they had spent more years in their current presidency than the normative group.

McFarlin, Crittenden, and Ebbers were cryptic with respect to how they divided their survey sample into their outstanding and normative groups, other than to say that the groupings were based upon peer ratings. Additionally, they did not report any data concerning the attitudes, values, and performance of the junior and community college presidents. Nonetheless, their work, though limited, did buttress Fisher, Tack, and Wheeler.

A significant study of college presidents was conducted by Birnbaum (1992) who, along with several colleagues, followed 32 presidents for almost five years in the late 1980s. Each president was interviewed twice during these years, and the Birnbaum team made on-site visits to each president's campus. A wide variety of other individuals connected to these presidents were interviewed, including governing board members, faculty, and the like. A total of 762 interviews were conducted, an impressive enterprise by any reasonable standard.

Birnbaum focused attention on the transformational versus transactional theories of presidential leadership and in essence arrived at the conclusion that "In the real world, there is almost never a simple yes or no answer..." (8). Birnbaum believes that leaders can make a difference, but only under certain conditions. Things that work on one campus may not work on another, he advises, and strategies that are appropriate to one time period may not be appropriate to another.

Birnbaum also critiqued what he termed "presidential myths." His five myths were:

1. *The Myth of Presidential Vision:* Even though it is frequently stated that successful presidents must possess an attractive vision, Birnbaum believes that most attractive visions were purloined and usually already existed on the campus. A successful president, he argues, simply finds that vision and exploits it.

2. *The Myth of the President as Transformational Leader:* Burns (1978) and others have contended that many of the problems of higher education

could be minimized or even solved if college presidents acted in a transformational fashion. However, as we have noted, Birnbaum believes this often leads to disruption and failure.

3. *The Myth of Presidential Charisma:* Charisma is, according to Birnbaum, a "mysterious ability" (31) and is exceedingly difficult to define. He believes that presidents who rely extensively on charisma fail to cultivate and utilize the internal workings of their institutions and rely too much on their personal savvy and ability to sway. Besides, he thinks that charisma can be and is used for evil purposes.

4. *The Myth of Presidential Distance:* Fisher (1984) argues that effective leaders maintain social distance. Based on his interviews and observations, Birnbaum says there is no support for this proposition.

5. *The Myth of President Style and Traits:* Birnbaum and his colleagues did not find any particular presidential style that uniformly results in success. In his words, "although some traits and skills appear frequently to be characteristics of leaders seen as effective, possession of such traits does not guarantee this effectiveness, nor does their absence proscribe it" (62–63). If there was a common thread that differentiated Birnbaum's effective presidents from the rest, it was their popularity—their standing with, and acceptance from, faculty, students, staff, alumni, and board members. However, many observers of the modern American college presidency, while hardly discounting presidential popularity as an important element, nevertheless regard personal popularity (metaphorically) as more of a thermometer than a furnace. Effective presidents often are (but need not be) popular; their popularity and ability to get along with their constituents, however, is usually not the primary source of their effectiveness.

Birnbaum is an experienced and highly published observer of higher education and college presidents, and his observations must be accorded respect. Yet his conclusions often are inconsistent with other empirical evidence. Further, they are highly dependent upon the impressions he and his colleagues divined from their interviews. As such, the evidence he presents is more normative than quantitative and is nonreplicable in a scientific sense. That is, no digitized data set exists, and no tests of statistical significance on specific hypotheses have been performed. Thus, his work is not verifiable.

A potential problem with normative studies of the college presidency (that is, with studies that do not have a statistically rigorous and replicable design) is that interviewers and observers may tend to hear and see what they expect (or want) to hear and see. All researchers, the authors of this study being no exception, must fight the intrusion of such biases into their work. It is not our contention that normative studies are useless.

Indeed, they have much to offer, and we supplement the statistical work we report in this study with interviews and observations from more than 100 institutions. Even so, as much as possible, we will progress in our knowledge of the college presidency if we test specific hypotheses, and our studies are replicable and have a scientific, empirical base.

That said, we agree that it will nearly always be easier for higher education experts to muse about the college presidency in a book or interview, and to offer educated conclusions about what makes higher education and college presidents tick, than it will be to collect reliable data about presidents and presidencies. We also acknowledge that there is room to question the accuracy of the data utilized in some empirical studies. It is possible that respondents may provide answers that reflect what they wish were true, or safe, noncontroversial responses, rather than the truth.

Nonetheless, in order to avoid the tyranny of unrepresentative individual anecdotes and impressionistic interviewing, we must also accumulate reliable, large-sample evidence in addition to normative studies. Only then can we check our impressions and the sage observations of experts with reliable empirical evidence.

Another essentially normative study of the American college presidency is that performed by Pruitt (1974), who looked at 25 presidents and reached conclusions about their personal and professional characteristics. Similarly, Bénezét, Katz, and Magnuson (1981) examined 25 institutions and their leaders, while Gilley et al. (1986) focused on 20 institutions they deemed to be especially innovative and successful. Plowman (1991) used survey data to study 25 Florida college presidents (18 independent, 7 public) to see if institutional environment influenced presidential behavior. He found no relationship, but he did discover that the Floridian presidents rated their own effectiveness much more highly than did their own senior administrative staff. Decades earlier, Bolman (1965), Ferrari (1970), and Gardner and Brown (1973) performed normative studies on varying samples of presidents.

Adjectives such as "dynamic," "energetic," "empowering," "wise," "flexible," "innovative," and "visionary" flow from the pages of all of these studies.[1] They are often very useful in describing the environment in which presidents toil and the numerous challenges and constraints they face. Despite these useful features, such studies do not yield firm, replicable statistical results in the tradition of Fisher, Tack, and Wheeler. This deficiency is especially common when former college presidents write idiosyncratically about their own institutions and presidencies. Usually, when we read such works, we are entertained, though not always enlightened in a scientific sense. We hasten to state that we believe there is room for both types of analyses as we seek an improved understanding of the nature of college presidencies in the United States. Yet our primary information deficit exists in the area of structured, statistical studies. The number of replicable, rigorous, large-sample statistical studies of the American college presidency can be counted on one hand, and hence that is where our greatest need for additional knowledge currently resides.

## RESISTANCE TO ENTREPRENEURIAL APPROACHES IN ACADEME

The term entrepreneurial sometimes evokes antipathy in higher education. Frequently, there is resistance to utilizing the term to describe activities inside colleges and universities. One reason for this is the origin of the word itself. The original gambling house connection of the word *entrepreneur* encouraged an interpretation of the word in some academic precincts that generated a mild distaste associated with things pedestrian, anti-intellectual, and even exploitative. Recent financial chicanery among apparently entrepreneurial American corporate leaders and corporations such as Enron and WorldCom undoubtedly has sharpened this sense of unease in the academy.

To some faculty, the adjective *entrepreneurial* manifests an objectionable vision of a nonacademic, profit-driven business firm that is uninterested in the traditional academic verities. Axelrod (2003) argues that "The ground is shifting beneath the contemporary university, and it is time to take stock of its precarious situation. The cultivation of intellect, long a central objective of university life, is threatened by political and economic pressures that are redefining and reshaping the functions of higher learning." Axelrod (108) believes that "self interest, conflict of interest, and commercial competition have the potential to warp academic culture." In this view, he is not alone. Marginson and Considine (2000, 237) argue that "Reinvention [i.e., entrepreneurial] strategies not underpinned by academic strength face severe limits...." The aversion of many academics to the value set they feel is implied by an entrepreneurial approach to higher education is part and parcel of a general distaste and suspicion that many academics harbor about the business world and commercialization.

Harvard's Emeritus President Derek Bok (2003b), whose own institution has participated heavily in entrepreneurial and commercialized ventures, has issued similar sentiments. He asks whether everything in a university is for sale, if the price is right. The answer he supplies is yes, all too often. He is particularly sensitive to possible conflicts of interest brought about by the commercial connections of universities. He scores the destructive possibilities of corporate and government-funded research that might threaten academic freedom and subtly bias results, university partnership investments in venture capital arrangements, industry-subsidized academic programs and centers that act as mouthpieces for industry views, and big-time intercollegiate athletics. In Bok's view, the siren song of entrepreneurial influences may lead to short-term gains for institutions of higher education, but it can have deleterious long-term effects.[2] Like Axelrod and others, he advocates that colleges and universities uphold academic values, even if this requires that they not pursue what appear to be profitable commercial avenues.

It is notable that the for-profit University of Phoenix has become the largest independent institution in the United States in terms of headcount enrollment but is questioned by certain faculty organizations such as the American Association of University Professors. Accrediting bodies such as the Southern Association of Colleges and Schools have also questioned some of Phoenix's unconventional measures. Correct or not, the prevailing faculty view is that such institutions utilize too many part-time faculty members, do not give sufficient heed to faculty rights and academic freedom, neglect library resources, and make curricular decisions on the basis of financial factors rather than what is academically appropriate. This is seen as entrepreneurship run amok and is perceived to be antithetical to the ideals of academe.

Despite the general prevalence of these views, some institutions of higher education and some presidents are unapologetic about their businesslike approach to higher education. Philadelphia's Drexel University has adopted what "is viewed by many as a 'corporate style' university with top-down leadership, quick decision making, and a focus on the bottom line" (Bielec, 2002, 9). Drexel's motto has become "Just Do It," and the institution boasts that freshmen admissions applications and its endowment have tripled, while undergraduate enrollment and research funding have doubled, both since 1995, when President Constantine Papadakis assumed the reins and vigorously changed the university's approach to the world. Nonetheless, this is an approach that Bok (2003b) and others warn against. "Unilateral decisions... are an invitation to trouble," argues Bok, who further comments that "enterprising presidents and deans are increasingly tempted to bypass faculty review when launching new entrepreneurial ventures" (191). Further, some activities require patient cultivation and cannot be rushed. As a cautious management expert once noted, it takes nine months to make a baby, no matter how many people one puts on the job.

In any case, the Drexels of the world appear to be the exception. In general, woe betide the college president who talks too openly about entrepreneurial activities, or for that matter about other related concepts such as risk taking in academic programming, economies of scale in academic programs, the rate of return on institutional investments in distance learning programs, or the price elasticity of demand of students for classroom seats. Not only will the typical faculty member not entirely understand such terms, but also many will denigrate their very use and application to academe.

As a faculty member sniffed to one of the authors several years ago, "There is a reason why Jesus drove the money changers out of the temple. They didn't belong there and neither does a balance sheet mentality in universities." She was walking arm in arm intellectually with an independent college governing board member who asserted that "We don't need entrepreneurs; what we need are presidents who are concerned about values and what is right and wrong." Recent episodes in big-time intercollegiate athletics hardly discourage these views.

Opinions such as these did not spring from virgin earth. Thorstein Veblen (1918) inveighed against university presidents who led their institutions in the direction of increased commercialization. Veblen charged that university presidents were prone to "malpractice" because of their connections to capitalism (286). No doubt Veblen would spin in his grave were he aware of the inroads of the marketplace on twenty-first-century academe. He charged that the typical college or university was morphing into a "corporation of learning" in which "the largest feasible output" was the goal rather than education (87–92). His contemporary, Upton Sinclair, who achieved far greater fame for his exposé of meatpacking, similarly declaimed that university presidents were fakers and liars whose function was "to travel about the country, and summon the kings and captains of finance, and dine in their splendid banquet halls" and later engage in predatory activities (Crowley, 1994, 102).

Yet, if a war has been fought over the soul of the university during the twentieth century, then even the ardent admirers of Veblen and Sinclair would agree that their legions have lost numerous battles, if not the war itself. No armistice has been declared, but the infusion of commercialization into modern academic institutions is widespread and, some would argue, almost irreversible.

## CHANGING TIMES, CIRCUMSTANCES, AND CAUSES

It goes almost without saying that we *do* need presidents who are concerned about students and faculty and who *do* know right from wrong. Yet the nature of the modern American college and university has changed significantly in recent years, and conditions now call for academic leaders who are the virtuous individuals the governing board member in the previous section desired, and much more. As the well-regarded 1996 Association of Governing Boards (AGB) study, *Renewing the Academic Presidency: Stronger Leadership for Tougher Times*, put it, the "capacity to respond to society's demands and at the same time protect scholarship is now threatened by society's unprecedented and conflicting demands on higher education. In today's era of massive change, colleges and universities need more effective, less encumbered presidential leadership..." (35). The AGB Report advises presidents to be "risk takers" and "change agents" (xi). They must do more than react to circumstances; they must mold the circumstances and shape the future.

The massive change that AGB believes is washing over higher education clearly includes significant transformations in the economic environment, which sometimes has mutated under the very feet of college presidents. Consequently, as Bok (2003b) and others have pointed out, the budget-cutting proclivities of state legislatures may have pushed some otherwise reluctant public university presidents into entrepreneurial modes. When an institution loses a significant portion of its budget, it is almost a certainty that it will give thought to alternatives, some of which may be commercial, in order to avoid painful cuts. Thus, public universities may privatize their food services, engage in research partnerships with corporations and government, and actively seek to sell services ranging from space and books to faculty consulting and topical workshops. Of course, this list of revenue- and profit-generating activities is only exemplary and could be much longer.

It does seem likely that budgetary difficulties have been a motivating factor in the entrepreneurial and commercial behavior of some public institutions. Yet it is not clear that there is any lesser degree of entrepreneurial activity in independent institutions, where state legislatures hold considerably less sway. Indeed, some of the major entrepreneurial ventures in modern higher education have occurred in independent institutions. Witness high-flying enterprises such as SRI International (formerly the Stanford Research Institute), which advertises on its Web site (www.sri.com) that it provides "valuable solutions to a wide range of clients" in a host of areas, or the multifaceted activities of the Media Laboratory at MIT. Indeed, MIT supports almost 300 major research centers and laboratories, nearly all of which have strong connections to industry and government. One of MIT's "alliances with industry" is a five-year, $35 million partnership with Du Pont (*Chronicle of Higher Education*, 2003).

How do we explain this? First, even independent institutions are dependent upon government for funding, whether for student tuition assistance and financial aid or for research and public service grants. Thus they are not immune to public budget crises. Second, and perhaps more important, independent institutions have more freedom of action than public institutions insofar as entrepreneurial activities are concerned. Typically, they are not afflicted by the stultifying, one-size-fits-all regulations that public institutions confront, or by the sometimes pernicious regulators who "guard" the public purse, or by the same intensity of political pressure on economic items that public universities often confront. It also remains true that most independent institutions have the opportunity to act more quickly, if they desire, than the typical public institution.

Of course, it would be inaccurate to overemphasize the different environments in which public and independent institutions play. It is fair to say that there has been some convergence in recent years between public and independent institutions, and the stark differences that once existed in several arenas have been modulated. Some public institutions (for example, the University of Virginia, where state appropriations have sagged perilously below 10 percent of the institution's total budget) increasingly look like independent institutions. Conversely, many independent institutions have become strongly dependent upon governmental appropriations and thus must dance to the regulator's tune if they wish to continue to receive such funds. Consider Johns Hopkins, which recorded a mere $999 million in research and development expenditures in 2001 (National Science Foundation, 2003). Convergence between independent and public institutions, then, is an ever more important phenomenon.

Other broad, almost generic stimuli resulting in increased academic entrepreneurialism include fuzziness concerning why universities really exist and the increasingly competitive atmosphere in higher education (Bok, 2003b). With respect to the fuzziness of missions, the issues of the *Chronicle of Higher Education* frequently echo debates over the soul of the academy and what tasks the professoriate should (or should not) undertake. It is fair to say that considerable disagreement exists. Nonetheless, as Bok has pointed out, the areas of the modern university where animal entrepreneurial spirits are most pronounced also are those disciplines and schools that appear to have achieved the greatest consensus about their missions. Engineers, scientists, and computer scientists, for example, frequently exhibit more agreement about what they should teach and what they should do than education faculty or religious studies professors. In fact, there may be continuing disagreement at a macro level over the purposes of universities writ large, but at the micro level within institutions there are many departments and even entire schools that manifest a generalized consensus, though perhaps not unanimity, concerning their respective lots in life. The typical electrical engineer, then, is not confused by his raison d'être, even though others within higher education may be.

The notion that increased competition in higher education has stimulated commercialized activity has surface appeal. An illustration is the area of student recruitment and admissions, where institutions now avidly court and compete for students in ways that were absolutely unheard-of 100 years ago. Even so, it is not clear which direction the causation runs in such instances. Does competition drive commercialization, or is it the other way around? Perhaps increased competition among institutions does promote commercialization. However, the reverse may also be true. Commercialization may stimulate competitive juices to flow because commercialized institutions are more sensitive to revenues and profits. In other words, causation appears to be joint.

Whatever the root causes of increased commercialization and entrepreneurial activity in the modern college and university, there is little argument that such phenomena assume much larger roles today than they did decades ago. For example, the University of Washington recorded more than $800 million in ongoing extramural research funding in 2003 (www.washington.edu), and it is apparent that higher education has become increasingly sensitive to external commercial pressures. In such a world, it cannot be a surprise that entrepreneurial risk taking by college presidents is bound to assume an increasingly important role.

## PRESIDENTIAL AND INSTITUTIONAL VISION

In order to be productive, college presidents ordinarily must have some type of plan to guide their actions, lest their presidencies gradually deteriorate into a mindless set of ad hoc adjustments to emerging circumstances. This plan or direction might come from the institution's mission, a strategic plan, a State of the College address by the president, or some other visible source. Each of these sources ideally contribute to, and should not contradict, the overriding vision that the president utilizes to drive and excite her colleagues and the institution.

Given the dynamic nature of modern society, effective presidents must be opportunistic and take advantage of new and seemingly unpredictable circumstances as they emerge. In that regard, strategic plans often serve as impediments because they may speak to a world that no longer exists. We are reminded of the public university where members of the governing board refused to countenance any presidential actions that were not supported explicitly by the university's two-year-old strategic plan. This was a recipe for disaster.

Yet how presidents and institutions react to changing circumstances is crucial. In the words of one president whom we interviewed as a part of this project, "Very few presidents achieve success as counterpunchers." In order to avoid excessively reactive, transactional presidencies, presidents must possess an operational and easily understood vision that informs and spurs their activities. Ideally, this "inspirational vision" (Whetten, 1984) captivates and energizes diverse campus constituencies by expressing cherished values and ideals and by motivating all involved to work cooperatively to attain levels of improvement previously thought impossible. It should expertly mix lofty goals and values with concrete objectives and implementation.

Few concepts in the literature of leadership have been more discussed (and dissected) than leadership vision. So sensitized did former American President George H.W. Bush become to charges that he lacked vision that he began to talk warily about "the vision thing," and this circumstance soon became the jocular object of *Saturday Night Live* episodes. Leaders who do not appear to possess an attractive and captivating vision are frequently criticized because the inference is that they are operating without a plan or a sense of the future of their organization. In the Book of Proverbs (29:18), the Bible says, "Where there is no vision, the people perish," and this has become an article of faith in both the religious and secular realms.

But there are visions and then there are visions. Limited visions that do not excite and energize constituents may be more disappointing to those concerned than having no vision at all. At least when no vision is expressed, there is always the chance that an excellent one might be on the way. Those being led frequently desire a grand vision that metaphorically lifts their gaze from their feet to the horizon.[3] Most campus constituents harbor a deep-seated desire to be a vital part of what once was termed "The Grandest of Enterprises" (Marshall, 1956). Faculty, staff, students, alumni, and friends thirst for leaders who are capable of creating and sustaining a vision that challenges and engages them in the pursuit of lofty goals and noble ends. The college president who is able to generate such a vision may well be astonished by the outpouring of commitment, effort, and innovation that issues forth from her colleagues and constituents. "I was bowled over by the energy and ideas that came from my faculty when we began to require practical internships and cooperative experiences of all of our undergraduate students," said a president whom we interviewed. "They produced great ideas we had never thought about," he marveled, and "they spent huge numbers of extra hours refining and implementing their proposals."

Attractive visions seldom involve the maintenance of the status quo. Those who seek to stand still in fact usually fall behind because of the dynamic nature of their environment. The rules of Latin grammar may not have changed much in the last 2000 years, but nearly everything else of consequence has been changing, sometimes at warp speed. Such a world requires an intelligent, well-devised activist response. Even an effective business leader such as former IBM CEO Lou Gerstner, who is alleged to have uttered that the last thing IBM needed was a vision, nonetheless had a vision. In Gerstner's case, his vision initially involved focusing his organization on its future and tightening, improving, extending, and eliminating many existing activities. Gerstner, despite his rhetoric, sold his colleagues and his stockholders on the notion that IBM needed to change and improve the way it was doing much of its business. His vision did not involve the status quo for IBM, and the title of his book describing this situation, *Who Says Elephants Can't Dance?* (Gerstner, 2002) underlines this. He acknowledged that he might be risking IBM's future with his decisions, but (like most successful leaders, inside and outside of higher education) he almost appeared to welcome the challenge implied.

There is an excitement and even romance associated with presidential visioning that recalls the observation of Karl Wallenda, the amazing high wire artist who risked his life hundreds of times: "Being on the tightrope is living; everything else is waiting" (Boone, 1992, 123). Presidents with successful visions often do live for their work and would not trade it for anything else, even though they may risk their positions and their reputations, and on occasion take abuse, because of their initiatives. Yet truly successful presidents do not only live for themselves; they simultaneously work prodigiously for their colleagues and their institutions. The best practitioners among this genre exhibit such a wonderful chemistry between individual ambition and group needs that they seldom receive long-term ad hominem criticism.

Nearly always, the implementation of a superb vision, and perhaps even its formation and explication, require entrepreneurial behavior on the part of the institution's president. Consequently, college presidents thought to possess attractive visions also tend to be those presidents who are innovative (entrepreneurial) (Fisher, Tack, and Wheeler, 1988). They are individuals who, in the words of Maletz and Katzenbach (2002, 118), "quickly become adept at operating in changing environments" and are unabashedly entrepreneurial.

In the view of some knowledgeable observers, however, the twenty-first century may have brought with it a tendency for many leaders to sidestep grand visions and instead to exhibit risk-averting behavior. One is reminded of the governor of Texas in the musical *Best Little Whorehouse in Texas*, who when faced with a serious issue, would sing, "Do a little side step," and then disappear. Some leaders attempt to talk the vision story, but do not walk it when push comes to shove. Jeffrey Garten, dean of the Yale School of Management, recently wrote disapprovingly that "the emerging virus in American business culture could be the penchant for playing it too safe—settling for nothing more than getting things done and gearing everything to meeting quarterly targets, while failing to exercise enough imagination about where to go and what to be" (Garten, 2003, 28). He forthrightly asserted that "There's still a requirement for chief executives to take educated risks," and they must understand that there is a need for them to be "thinking about how to make the future better and placing bets on [their] vision" (28).

## TRANSFORMATIONAL PRESIDENCIES IMPLY RISK-TAKING BEHAVIOR

Presidents seeking to transform their institutions must be willing to take intelligent risks and to engage in entrepreneurial activity. A president who does not take some risks is a president who likely accomplishes nothing, or at least nothing more than would have happened in her absence. Such a president might well fit into the Cohen and March, or Birnbaum models.

Gilley et al. (1986) examined 20 institutions "on the move" and found impressive evidence not only that the presidents of these institutions possessed attractive and highly motivating visions, but also that they were the source of innovative, outside-the-box proposals and solutions. These presidents were risk takers in the true sense of the term, for both they and their institutions chanced failure if the innovations did not prove productive. Gilley's onetime colleague, George Johnson, provokingly observed that successful presidents "should seize every opportunity to cause trouble, to make the conventional path more trouble than the unconventional one" (Fisher and Tack, 1988, 69). Johnson, a long-time president of George Mason University, was a firm believer in the principle that it is necessary to break a few eggs in order to make a good omelet. Observers from the corporate sector typically exhibit similar sentiments. To achieve success, advise Hamel and Skarzynski (2002, 13), companies must "abandon old rules, shed old habits, and upend cherished conventions," while Hesselbein (2002) argues that institutions must peel away their old hierarchy, challenge existing assumptions, promote flexibility, and sometimes strike out into the unknown in order to thrive. Thus, transformational leaders (academic or corporate) must be willing to break the mold, do things differently, even court revolution at times, and take risks.

## THE NOTION OF PRUDENT RISKS

As one of the authors' faculty mentors once put it, "Some alternatives might be risky, while others are *really* risky. You need to know which is which." By this, he meant that in many situations, there is a continuum of risky alternatives from which one might choose. Attached to each alternative on the menu of possibilities is a potential set of rewards and costs, as well as a probability distribution describing how likely (or unlikely) each occurrence is. Yet these may not be known with certainty, and hence some alternatives inherently are more risky than others.

In fact, in some situations, college presidents may not know which alternatives exist, much less how likely they are to occur. This is most apt to be true for inexperienced presidents, and it is one reason why empirical studies of presidential effectiveness typically find that experienced presidents are more effective than those less experienced. A new president who is a chemist may not understand perfectly the needs and problems of the humanities, and vice versa. The chief academic officer who has just risen to his first presidency initially may not have command of specific financial topics and may not even understand what questions to ask. Hence, it is a challenge for such individuals to engage in prudent decision making, and frequently they must depend heavily upon the judgment of others when risky alternatives present themselves.

Regardless, the essence of entrepreneurial success is the taking of prudent risks. This implies intelligent, rational assessment of alternatives. This assessment may or may not be quantitative. The most important questions that bedevil higher education today (for example, the use of technology to increase learning or to achieve larger mean class sizes) frequently revolve at least as much around values as numbers. Thus, deciding *what* should be done often is a more critical part of the decision process than determining *how* it should be done. *What* should be done usually depends upon the hierarchy of presidential and institutional values. Are small, intimate undergraduate class sections more important than a top 20 ranking in an academic discipline such as physics? If the cost of achieving each goal were identical, which course should the institution pursue? Much depends upon the presidential and institutional *Weltanschauung*—their view of what really counts in the world.

Prudent risk taking, then, means that the decision maker must understand her own values and priorities, delineate available alternatives and their likelihood of occurrence, and accurately assess the benefits and costs associated with each alternative. Prudence implies intelligent, calculating decision making, given the circumstances. Prudent risk taking may be data driven; it is always value driven.

Entrepreneurial presidents (and perhaps those presidents who are effective in the Fisher, Tack, and Wheeler context) are prudent risk takers who seldom, if ever, make truly important decisions without appropriate analysis and forethought. They may appear to make quick decisions and snap judgments, but only because they have usually thought about such matters many times previously and are confident both of their own values and their approach to the world. This enables them to be prompt, decisive, and timely. By such means, they inspire confidence and transform their institutions.

Contrast transformational presidents with transactional presidents, who seldom assume risks of any consequence, either for their institutions or for themselves. Frequently, they overanalyze situations, waver among alternatives, delay their decisions, and ultimately seek to protect themselves by taking a vote among their senior officers or constituents. Transactional presidents are known for explaining to exasperated governing boards seeking action and improvement that, "This is what the campus wants." They seek overwhelming consensus (which no one would deny is preferable to division), though often at the cost of timely action. Consequently, they are seldom entrepreneurial. If their institutions are quite well situated, possess large endowments, and are lucky enough not be faced with major crises, these presidents will complete their service without tragedy or explosion. Because they have not antagonized any major constituency, often they are well regarded and fêted upon their retirement from the presidency. Their institutions, however, acquire inertia and slowly, incrementally garner the reputation of being dead in the water. In a world characterized by accelerating change, this can be a dangerous circumstance for both leader and institution.

According to Peter Drucker and Peter Senge, change is not perceived as a threat by prudent risk takers (Hesselbein and Johnston, 2002b). "Change is an opportunity and not a threat," say these well-known management gurus (11). "If people are enjoying their work, they'll innovate, they'll take risks, they'll trust one another because they are committed to what they're doing" (15). Change and risk taking, then, must be infused into an organization's culture in such a fashion that the intelligent analysis and management of risk, and subsequent capitalization upon the opportunities presented, becomes second nature to the organization. Prudent risk taking is a daily consideration that should not require emergency meetings and elevated blood pressure.

## THE NEXUS OF THIS STUDY

The sometimes discordant views of leadership and the college presidency that we have sketched in this chapter provoke two critical questions:

1. Do college presidents really have the power and influence to develop a vision, encourage entrepreneurial initiatives, assume intelligent risks, and thereby transform their institutions?
2. If these things are possible, can college presidents really do them with a degree of success that we can measure?

Suffice it to say that there is disagreement about such things among those who have studied the college presidency. Nonetheless, these questions are primarily empirical in nature, and we provide evidence concerning them in this study.

# CHAPTER

# Matters of Process: The Survey and the Data

A difference of opinion is what makes horse racing and missionaries.
—Will Rogers

Prejudice saves a lot of time, because you can form an opinion without the facts.

—Anonymous

In January 2002, we wrote to more than 1,500 college and university presidents, heads of accrediting bodies, chairpersons of disciplinary associations, and chief executive officers of state higher education coordinating bodies to ask them to help us identify "especially effective, especially successful" college presidents. Our letter to these individuals is reproduced in Appendix A. We utilized the 2002 edition of the *Higher Education Directory* (Rodenhouse, 2001) to identify the individuals who received our request. Every third sitting college president (about 1,300) received our letter, and each head or chair of a major regional or disciplinary accrediting body also received the letter, as did all chief executive officers of state higher education agencies. In addition, we sent letters to approximately two dozen other prominent individuals who recently retired from their presidencies, or whose scholarly work on related subjects has often appeared in recent years.

All of the 1,517 individuals who received our letter requesting nominations occupied (or recently did occupy) a strategic position in higher education. They were well positioned to be knowledgeable about the performance and effectiveness of sitting college presidents. We refer to these 1,517 individuals as our experts, for they are better situated to evaluate America's college presidents than any other available constituency. The broad characteristics of these experts are described in Table 3.1.

In our letter to the experts, we noted that "the first statistically rigorous and replicable empirical study of what makes some college presidents more effective and successful than others" had been conducted by James L. Fisher, Martha W. Tack, and Karen J. Wheeler (1988) about 15 years earlier. Now, we pointed out, with the support of the Kauffman Foundation, we were testing and expanding that study by focusing specially upon entrepreneurial presidents. But we also pointed out that we intended to give additional attention to women and minority presidents, whose ranks had swelled considerably in recent years. We asked each expert to nominate up to six sitting college and university presidents who were particularly effective and successful in their positions. Former presidents were not eligible. Further, individuals who did not then occupy a presidential position (for example, provosts, vice presidents, chairs of governing boards, elected political figures) were not eligible, either. We attached a self-addressed, stamped envelope to expedite their replies.

Ultimately, we received 529 nominating letters in which 701 college and university presidents were nominated. In about 1 percent of the cases, individuals nominated themselves, and in about 2 percent of the cases, individuals were nominated who were not eligible because they were not a sitting college or university president. The general characteristics of the nominated presidents are reported in Table 3.2.

Table 3.1
The Identity of the Experts Asked for Nominations

| | |
|---|---|
| Sitting Presidents of American Colleges and Universities | 1,298 |
| Heads of Regional and National Accrediting Agencies | 141 |
| Heads of State Higher Education Authorities and Coordinating Bodies | 51 |
| Nationally Recognized Authorities Not Included Above | 27 |
| Total | 1,517 |

Table 3.2
Characteristics of Presidents Nominated as Effective and Successful

| | |
|---|---|
| Total Number of Presidents Nominated | 701 |
| • Men | 533 (76.0%) |
| • Women | 168 (24.0%) |
| **Major Institutional Types** | |
| • Located at Public Institution | 388 (55.3%) |
| • Located at Independent Institution | 313 (44.7%) |
| • Liberal Arts College or University | 230 (32.8%) |
| • Two Year Institution | 198 (28.2%) |
| • Research Institution (Carnegie) | 116 (16.6%) |
| • Historically Black College or University | 42 (6.0%) |
| • Proprietary Institution | 22 (3.1%) |
| (overlap between institutional types exists) | |
| Census Region in Which Nominee Resides | |
| • Northeast | 144 (21.6%) |
| • Midwest | 218 (32.5%) |
| • South | 202 (30.1%) |
| • West | 106 (15.8%) |

## DISTRIBUTING AND COLLECTING THE SURVEY

In March 2002, we wrote to every eligible nominated president and asked him/her to complete and return to us a detailed survey instrument. This survey instrument is attached in Appendix B and contained 82 separate requests for data and 187 possible responses. We believe it to be the most detailed survey instrument ever administered to a large group of college presidents.

Both of the authors spent many years as college presidents and therefore know well the constant pressures on presidential time. Therefore, we were not sanguine about our prospects to elicit a heavy response from the 701 nominated presidents. Many presidents believe that they have better things to do with their time.[1] Nonetheless, 382 (54.5 percent) of these presidents did respond to our letter (which is reproduced in Appendix C) and returned the survey. Of these returned surveys, 371 (97.1 percent) were usable.

From the 371 presidents nominated as especially successful who returned usable surveys, 10 different experts nominated one paragon. However, as Table 3.3 reveals, 241 were nominated only once, while the remaining 130 presidents were nominated more than once.

Hereafter, we label this group of 371 nominated, returned survey presidents as our effective presidents. Whether they *actually* are effective and

Table 3.3
Frequency of Nominations of Presidents as Effective and Successful by the
Experts

| NUMBER OF NOMINATIONS | NUMBER OF PRESIDENTS RECEIVING THIS NUMBER OF NOMINATIONS |
|:---:|:---:|
| 1 | 241 |
| 2 | 97 |
| 3 | 6 |
| 4 | 9 |
| 5 | 3 |
| 6 | 2 |
| 7 | 1 |
| 8 | 0 |
| 9 | 1 |
| 10 | 1 |

successful in their presidencies is a classic beauty-is-in-the-eye-of-the-viewer proposition. Alas, no definitive, agreed-upon definition of presidential effectiveness exists. In fact, there is much disagreement in the literature about what effective presidents should do (or should not do), to say nothing of the argument over whether they have the power to do much of consequence, even if they urgently wanted to do so. As we saw in chapter 2, much of the discussion concerning transformational versus transactional leadership relates to substantive disagreements about these matters.

Deliberately, we did not specify what we meant by presidential effectiveness and success when we asked individuals for nominations. Our letter forthrightly stated, "Please use your own definition of effectiveness." We marched down this path for two reasons. First, there is disagreement on the subject, and any definition that we might have supplied could have generated both criticism and nonparticipation. We did not want respondents to say, "I disagree with this approach and so I won't participate." Therefore, and second, we were interested in what knowledgeable individuals (experts) perceive presidential effectiveness to be. At least somewhat, presidential effectiveness devolves into a set of empirical questions. What do experts perceive effectiveness to be (as evidenced by the characteristics of the individuals they nominate)? What are the actual characteristics of these effective individuals vis-à-vis the representative presidents? Further, how can we connect these perceptions to real-world magnitudes such as enrollment, institutional quality, endowments, presidential behavior, and the like?

Broadly speaking, many parts of our survey instrument replicated the Fisher/Tack/Wheeler instrument from the 1980s, primarily because we were interested in seeing if presidential backgrounds, attitudes, and behavior have changed since that time. But we also added items to the survey that specifically dealt with the following topics:

Entrepreneurial presidents (a topic to which we will return)

Presidential use of, and reliance upon, modern technologies such as computers, cell telephones, and the Internet

Presidential academic backgrounds in areas such as accounting, computer science, and economics

## CONTROL AND PERFORMANCE DATA

A variety of scholarly ventures have examined the college presidency and have offered surmises about what constitutes effectiveness in that position. In these discussions, attention often has centered upon difficult-to-measure notions such as presidential popularity and acceptance by groups such as faculty. Yet, absent obvious manifestations such as a no-confidence motion by the Faculty Senate or a public chastisement or termination of the president by his board, who *really* knows how popular and accepted a college president is? More than one president beloved by the community has been abhorred by her faculty, and vice versa. Presidential popularity is difficult to measure and is an elusive commodity. The bottom line is that there are no accepted measures of presidential popularity and, even more important, no database one might utilize.

Alternatively, in discussions of presidential effectiveness, some attention has been given to measurable, though frequently elusive, concepts such as enhanced presidential and institutional reputation. Here, much public attention (some say grossly excessive attention) has been given to measures such as the annual *U.S. News and World Report* rankings of institutions. However, there has been no empirical work connecting those ratings to presidential effectiveness. Still another alternative is to focus upon more easily measurable magnitudes such as enrollment and endowment growth, the theory being that these could constitute a scoreboard for presidential effectiveness.

Each of these alternatives carries with it strengths and weaknesses, and we will discuss these in a later chapter. Nonetheless, in principle we were committed to an attempt to link *perceived presidential effectiveness* (and that is what our nominations reflect) with *actual measures of performance*. This has never been done in previous studies except on an individual, anecdotal basis.

Accordingly, we collected information about each president's institution in each of the following general areas:

Carnegie institutional classification

Headcount enrollment and enrollment growth

Endowment size and growth

Alumni and donor giving magnitudes

Size of operating budget

*U.S. News and World Report* institutional prestige ranking

Student body characteristics, including gender, age and minority status, and
their performance on standardized tests such as the ACT or SAT

Note that since these data are not available for all institutions, the empirical work that we report that relies upon such variables necessarily involves reduced sample sizes. For example, easily the most utilized source for endowment information and fund-raising activity is the annual report of the Council for Aid to Education (CAE). However, many institutions (mostly smaller in size) choose not to report their fund-raising activities to the CAE, and therefore their data are not available unless one has a specific contact on that campus. A notable example of lack of data availability relates to the annual *U.S. News and World Report* prestige rating. *U.S. News* does not rate junior and community colleges, and similarly it does not rate for-profit institutions, both of which are contained in our survey. This means that even if our performance measures are faultless, they still will describe only portions of the diverse higher education spectrum. Thus, the power of our conclusions in this arena will be diminished.

Finally, it always will be difficult to separate individual presidents from their institutions. Is President Smith really responsible for State U's increased enrollment, or might this have happened in any case, almost regardless of who was the president? Whether institutional data (for an entire college or university) accurately reflect presidential performance is arguable and underpins much of the discussion concerning transformational versus transactional presidential models. It is not unlike attempting to divine if the coach of a winning basketball team is the guiding light who is responsible for that success, or instead the wins have little to do with him and are primarily a function of the players on the team's roster. We acknowledge the potential difficulty associated with separating institutions from presidents, but we regard it as a challenge rather than as an absolute barrier to statistical analysis. There are statistical means such as multivariate analysis to control for institutional influences, and we will utilize them in later chapters.

# THE CONTROL GROUP: THE REPRESENTATIVE PRESIDENTS

The essence of our project is to compare our effective (nominated) presidents with representative (unnominated) presidents. We want to know how the effective presidents differ from the representative presidents (if at all) in background, attitudes, values, behavior, and performance. Consequently, we had to assemble a large group of representative presidents. This is not so easily accomplished if the individuals concerned come to realize that they are not part of the effective president group. Therefore, without indicating whether the recipient had been nominated or not, we sent surveys to 1,289 unnominated presidents and asked for their help in assembling data about American college and university presidents. A copy of the letter to the representative presidents is reproduced in Appendix D. Three hundred forty-nine (27.1 percent) responded, and 342 (98.0 percent) provided us with usable surveys. Hence, our ultimate sample consisted of 371 effective presidents and 342 representative presidents. Table 3.4 summarizes these data.

# A MORE DETAILED ANALYSIS OF THE SURVEY INSTRUMENT

The survey instrument, which is reproduced in Appendix B, contained eight distinct sections:

1. *Professional Education Relating to the President.* Each president was provided with the opportunity to supply his/her educational status and the source of his/her academic degrees. In addition, each president was asked to provide us with data relating to the amount of coursework he/she had taken in the areas of accounting, computer science, economics, and statistics. Finally, we asked the presidents to tell us their gender, ethnic background, and age.

Table 3.4
Presidents Who Completed the Survey Instrument

| CHARACTERISTIC | NUMBER OF PRESIDENTS |
|---|---|
| Nominated as being Effective and Successful | 371 |
| Not Nominated | 342 |

2. *Basic Demographic Data.* We asked each president to supply us with his/her basic demographic data: age, gender, and ethnic background.

3. *Previous Positions Held by the President and Presidential Experience.* We asked all of our presidents to trace their higher education careers for us, beginning with their first position in higher education and culminating in their current position. We also asked the presidents to tell us when they assumed their presidency, the position they held when appointed to this presidency, and how much experience they had outside of higher education.

4. *Presidential Reliance upon Technology.* In this section, we asked the presidents to tell us the extent to which they utilize technology such as computers, the Internet, and cell telephones, both personally and to maintain contact with those who report to them.

5. *Presidential Scholarly Activity.* Presidents were asked to inform us of the number of books and scholarly articles they had published, their number of professional organization memberships, the organizations in which they participated most frequently, and any offices held in those organizations.

6. *Politics and Religion.* Here, the presidents in our sample were asked to tell us of their political or religious preferences.

7. *Family Characteristics.* This section focused upon the family characteristics of the president, including the educational attainment of his/her father and mother, marital status, and the number and ages of his/her children. In addition, we asked the presidents to tell us about the activities of their spouses or significant others. Finally, we asked each president to tell us the region of their birth and where they currently resided.

8. *Personal Attitudes and Leadership Styles.* Each president responded to 60 statements by means of a conventional five-response Likert scale. For example, in response to the statement, "I am sometimes viewed as hard-nosed," each president could indicate one of the following five levels of agreement: "Strongly Agree," "Agree," "Undecided," "Disagree," and "Strongly Disagree." Eleven of the 60 statements explicitly focused upon the entrepreneurial attitudes and activities of the president.

## DATA SOURCES

The sources of all data not derived from the survey instrument are described in Appendix E.

# CHAPTER 4

## The 713 Presidents in Our Sample: A Profile and Statistical Tests

Research is the process of going up alleys to see if they are blind.
 —Marston Bates, twentieth-century American zoologist

It is a capital mistake to theorize before one has data.
 —Sir Arthur Conan Doyle

If you torture the data long enough, they will confess.
 —Anonymous

The 713 presidents in our sample are broadly representative of the population of all presidents of colleges and universities in the United States. There exists one very important external reality check for this assertion. Every three to four years, the American Council on Education's Center for Policy Analysis conducts a valuable demographic survey of American college presidents. The most recent version, incorporating data from 2,594 presidents, was published in 2002 (American Council on Education, 2002). The ACE survey is more detailed than ours in several areas (an example being the various forms of compensation presidents receive and the perquisites they enjoy), but much less detailed in others because it is not directed at presidential attitudes, values, and behavior, which are our focus. The two surveys were designed for different purposes. The ACE survey is designed to be descriptive, while ours is designed to permit inferences about attitudes, value, and behavior.

That said, the 2002 ACE data are quite consistent with those we report in Table 4.1. For example, the ACE found the mean age of its presidents to be 57.5, while we find the mean age to be 57.18. Of ACE's presidents, 21.1 percent were women and 12.8 percent were minorities, while the comparable numbers in our survey are 19.1 percent and 11.2 percent, respectively. The ACE data, which were generated from a sample of the more than 4,000 presidents nationally, lend confidence to the notion that our sample is a reasonable depiction of the population of higher education presidents.[1]

Table 4.1 also reveals interesting differences between effective and representative presidents that we will explore in greater detail. We find our effective presidents to be older, more experienced, more likely to hold a doctorate, more likely to be located at a research institution, politically more liberal, less likely to have spent time outside of higher education, and less likely to believe in organizational structure. As we shall see, the gap between effective presidents and representative presidents is especially pronounced with respect to their entrepreneurial instincts and behavior. Effective presidents are substantially more entrepreneurial than representative presidents.

However, before we give the data in Table 4.1 a closer inspection, we must point out that college presidents as a group are hardly typical Americans. College presidents are better educated, earn higher incomes, are much more heavily male and Caucasian, and are politically more liberal than the nonpresidential population. For example, more than 80 percent of the presidents in our sample are male, whereas slightly less than one-half of the American population is male. Eighty-five percent of our presidents are Caucasian, though only 77 percent of the American population is Caucasian (U.S. Census Bureau, 2003a). Only 26 percent of our presidents say they are Republicans politically, while more than 40 percent of individuals nationally label themselves Republicans (Harris Interactive, 2003). Thus, it is fair to say that college presidents are distinctive, perhaps unusual individuals. Many generalizations that apply to the citizenry at large do not apply to college presidents (and perhaps to many other individuals who occupy key leadership roles in society). By virtue of their training, backgrounds, and choice of vocation, college presidents are a distinctive group.

## THE DATA

Table 4.1 records the mean responses of effective and representative presidents to a broad range of queries and includes control group data relating

Table 4.1
Mean Presidential Characteristics: Effective, Representative and Overall

| | **N** | **All** | **Effec-tive** | **Repre-sentative** | **Statistical Probability Attached to Difference*** |
|---|---|---|---|---|---|
| Age | 688 | 57.18 | 57.65 | 56.68 | .049e |
| Age on Becoming a President | 667 | 46.58 | 45.46 | 47.79 | .000e |
| Female | 136 | 19.1% | 16.4% | 21.9% | .000c |
| Male | 577 | 80.9% | 83.6% | 78.1% | .000c |
| Caucasian | 606 | 85.0% | 85.4% | 84.5% | .054c |
| African-American | 33 | 4.6% | 5.9% | 3.2% | .000c |
| Asian-American | 3 | 0.4% | 0.3% | 0.6% | SSI |
| Hispanic | 30 | 4.2% | 2.4% | 6.1% | .000c |
| Native American | 14 | 2.0% | 1.9% | 2.0% | SSI |
| Other or Unidentified | 27 | 3.8% | 4.0% | 3.5% | SSI |
| Roman Catholic | 153 | 21.5% | 19.9% | 23.1% | .000c |
| Methodist | 111 | 15.6% | 14.8% | 16.4% | .006c |
| Presbyterian | 75 | 10.5% | 10.8% | 10.2% | .071c |
| Baptist | 60 | 8.4% | 9.7% | 7.0% | .000c |
| Lutheran | 47 | 6.6% | 6.5% | 6.7% | .866c |
| Other Protestant | 83 | 11.6% | 11.1% | 12.3% | .121c |
| Jewish | 28 | 3.9% | 3.8% | 4.1% | SSI |
| Muslim | 0 | 0.0% | 0.0% | 0.0% | SSI |
| Other or Unidentified | 156 | 21.9% | 23.4% | 20.2% | .000c |
| Hold a Doctorate | 652 | 91.4% | 96.5% | 86.0% | .000c |
| If the President holds a doctorate, it is: | | | | | |
| From a Public Institution | 357 | 50.1% | 52.9% | 47.1% | .000c |
| • Ph.D. | 415 | 63.7% | 69.8% | 56.1% | .000c |
| • Ed.D. | 158 | 24.2% | 20.4% | 28.9% | .000c |
| • J.D. | 42 | 6.5% | 5.3% | 7.8% | .000c |
| • M.D | 5 | 0.8% | 0.3% | 1.4% | SSI |
| • Other | 32 | 4.9% | 4.2% | 5.8% | .000c |
| • In Business | 13 | 2.0% | 1.7% | 2.4% | SSI |
| • In Education | 252 | 38.9% | 34.9% | 43.2% | .000c |
| • In Engineering | 8 | 1.2% | 1.4% | 1.0% | SSI |
| • In Humanities or Fine Arts | 134 | 20.6% | 19.0% | 22.4% | .000c |

(continued)

Table 4.1
(Continued)

| | | | | | |
|---|---|---|---|---|---|
| • In Law | 29 | 4.4% | 4.2% | 4.8% | SSI |
| • In Medicine or Health Sci. | 12 | 1.8% | 1.7% | 2.0% | SSI |
| • In Sciences or Mathematics | 40 | 6.1% | 6.4% | 5.8% | .023$c$ |
| • In Social or Behavioral Sci. | 68 | 10.4% | 10.6% | 10.2% | .001$c$ |
| • In Some Other Area | 96 | 14.7% | 20.1% | 8.2% | .000$c$ |
| Hold Baccalaureate Degree | 677 | 95.0% | 96.4% | 93.3% | .000$c$ |
| Received Baccalaureate Degree from Public Institution | 177 | 51.7% | 49.4% | 54.2% | .000$c$ |
| Have taken two or more courses in economics | 354 | 49.6% | 49.1% | 50.3% | .226$c$ |
| Have taken two or more courses in statistics | 437 | 61.3% | 62.2% | 60.2% | .020$c$ |
| Have taken two or more courses in accounting | 152 | 21.3% | 18.9% | 24.0% | .000$c$ |
| Have taken two or more courses in computer science | 179 | 25.1% | 21.8% | 28.7% | .000$c$ |
| Hold Honorary Degrees | 102 | 14.3% | 18.3% | 9.9% | .000$c$ |
| Number of Published Books | 713 | 1.21 | 1.44 | .97 | .000$e$ |
| Number of Published Refereed Journal Articles | 713 | 12.63 | 14.37 | 10.75 | .000$e$ |
| Years as a President | 683 | 10.3 | 11.8 | 8.6 | .000$e$ |
| Years in Current Presidency | 688 | 8.1 | 9.5 | 6.6 | .000$e$ |
| Years Outside Higher Education | 536 | 7.2 | 6.0 | 8.6 | .000$e$ |
| Prior to becoming a president, I: | | | | | |
| No Response | 18 | 2.5% | 2.7% | 2.3% | SSI |
| Was outside of higher education | 57 | 11.6% | 5.4% | 10.8% | .000$c$ |
| Was inside higher education | 638 | 89.5% | 91.9% | 86.8% | .000$c$ |
| • Was a Provost, Vice Chancellor, or Vice President in a College or University | 518 | 72.7% | 72.5% | 72.8% | .808$c$ |
| • Was in Academic Affairs | 536 | 84.0% | 83.4% | 84.7% | .031$c$ |
| • Was in Institutional Advancement | 32 | 5.1% | 5.3% | 4.7% | .084$c$ |
| • Was in Student Affairs | 38 | 5.9% | 6.2% | 5.6% | .081$c$ |
| • Was in Administration and Finance | 10 | 1.6% | 1.5% | 1.7% | SSI |
| • Was in another area or no response | 22 | 3.5% | 3.6% | 3.3% | SSI |

(continued)

Table 4.1
(Continued)

| | | | | | |
|---|---|---|---|---|---|
| Political Independent | 223 | 31.2% | 35.3% | 26.9% | .000c |
| Political Democrat | 262 | 36.7% | 36.6% | 36.8% | .814c |
| Political Republican | 186 | 26.0% | 20.5% | 32.2% | .000c |
| Political Other | 7 | 1.0% | 0.8% | 1.2% | SSI |
| Unidentified | 35 | 4.9% | 6.8% | 2.9% | .000c |
| Never Married | 40 | 5.6% | 5.1% | 6.1% | .022c |
| Currently Divorced | 40 | 5.6% | 5.1% | 6.1% | .022c |
| Currently Widowed | 11 | 1.5% | 2.4% | 0.5% | SSI |
| Currently Married | 590 | 82.7% | 81.9% | 83.6% | .000c |
| Marital Status Not Identified | 32 | 4.4% | 5.5% | 3.7% | .000c |
| Spouse Is Employed Full-Time | 227 | 31.8% | 30.2% | 33.6% | .000c |
| Spouse Is Employed Part-Time | 115 | 16.1% | 17.0% | 15.2% | .004c |
| Spouse Is Compensated By Institution | 51 | 7.2% | 9.2% | 5.0% | .000c |
| Spouse Contributes Uncompensated Time | 417 | 58.4% | 61.7% | 55.0% | .000c |
| Spouse Does Not Attend Many Campus Events | 101 | 14.2% | 11.1% | 17.5% | .000c |
| Number of Children | 664 | 2.2% | 2.2% | 2.3% | .095c |
| Age Youngest Child | 593 | 24.6% | 25.6% | 26.5% | .036c |
| Born in Northeast U.S. | 134 | 18.8% | 18.6% | 19.0% | .441c |
| Born in Midwest U.S. | 185 | 25.9% | 24.5% | 27.5% | .009c |
| Born in South U.S. | 163 | 22.9% | 25.9% | 19.6% | .000c |
| Born in West U.S. | 57 | 8.0% | 6.7% | 9.4% | .000c |
| Born Elsewhere or Unidentified | 174 | 24.4% | 24.3% | 24.5% | .331c |
| Live in Northeast U.S. | 124 | 17.4% | 16.4% | 18.4% | .000c |
| Live in Midwest U.S. | 187 | 26.2% | 25.9% | 26.6% | .163c |
| Live in South U.S. | 234 | 32.8% | 37.7% | 27.5% | .000c |
| Live in West U.S. | 122 | 17.1% | 14.3% | 20.2% | .000c |
| Live Elsewhere or Unidentified | 46 | 6.5% | 5.7% | 7.3% | .000c |
| Father's Education: | | | | | |
| Less Than High School | 164 | 23.1% | 24.5% | 21.3% | .000c |
| Some High School | 52 | 7.6% | 6.2% | 8.4% | .000c |
| High School Diploma | 154 | 25.9% | 22.9% | 23.2% | .000c |
| College Courses | 94 | 13.2% | 12.1% | 14.3% | .000c |
| Baccalaureate Degree | 105 | 15.0% | 12.1% | 17.5% | .000c |
| Post-Baccalaureate Courses | 16 | 2.5% | 1.3% | 3.2% | SSI |
| Master's Degree | 57 | 8.2% | 9.4% | 6.4% | .000c |
| Doctoral Degree | 40 | 5.7% | 6.4% | 4.6% | .000c |

(continued)

Table 4.1
(Continued)

| | N | All | | Repre-sentative | |
|---|---|---|---|---|---|
| Post-Doctoral Work | 8 | 1.5% | 0.5% | 1.8% | SSI |
| No Response | 23 | 3.6% | 4.3% | 2.0% | SSI |
| Mother's Education: | | | | | |
| Less Than High School | 97 | 13.8% | 14.6% | 12.6% | .000c |
| Some High School | 38 | 5.8% | 4.0% | 6.7% | .000c |
| High School Diploma | 269 | 37.7% | 38.2% | 37.1% | .004c |
| College Courses | 115 | 16.2% | 15.6% | 16.7% | .009c |
| Baccalaureate Degree | 99 | 13.9% | 13.7% | 14.0% | .252c |
| Post-Baccalaureate Courses | 11 | 1.6% | 1.9% | 1.2% | SSI |
| Master's Degree | 51 | 7.2% | 6.4% | 7.9% | .000c |
| Doctoral Degree | 11 | 1.6% | 1.3% | 1.8% | SSI |
| Post-Doctoral Work | 0 | 0.0% | 0.0% | 0.0% | SSI |
| No Response | 22 | 3.3% | 4.0% | 2.0% | SSI |
| Published Annual Salary (000s) | 590 | $161 | $178 | $143 | .000e |

**Presidential Attitudes and Values**

In my own estimation, I:

(5 = strongly agree; 4 = agree; 3 = undecided; 2 = disagree; 1 = strongly disagree

| | | N | All | Effec-tive | Repre-sentative | Statistical Probability Attached to Difference* |
|---|---|---|---|---|---|---|
| 1) | Am sometimes viewed as hard-nosed | 713 | 3.60 | 3.62 | 3.57 | .431n |
| 2) | Believe that respect from those I lead is crucial | 713 | 4.69 | 4.73 | 4.66 | .205e |
| 3) | Believe that an effective leader takes risks | 713 | 4.70 | 4.73 | 4.67 | .287e |
| 4) | Place a high value on consensus | 713 | 3.97 | 4.02 | 3.92 | .090e |
| 5) | Believe in organizational structure | 713 | 4.09 | 3.98 | 4.21 | .000n |
| 6) | Believe that the leader should be perceived as self-confident | 713 | 4.53 | 4.55 | 4.51 | .586n |
| 7) | Believe in close collegial relationships with faculty | 713 | 3.84 | 3.80 | 3.87 | .205e |
| 8) | Believe that a leader serves the people | 713 | 4.46 | 4.41 | 4.51 | .090e |
| 9) | Believe in merit pay | 713 | 3.98 | 4.02 | 3.94 | .162n |
| 10) | Am sometimes viewed as assertive | 713 | 4.19 | 4.21 | 4.16 | .431n |
| 11) | Frequently violate the status quo | 713 | 3.84 | 3.92 | 3.75 | .019e |

(continued)

Table 4.1
(Continued)

| | | | | | |
|---|---|---|---|---|---|
| 12) Delegate responsibility and authority to subordinates | 713 | 4.55 | 4.55 | 4.56 | .916$n$ |
| 13) Believe in the value of one-on-one meetings | 713 | 4.49 | 4.48 | 4.51 | .646$n$ |
| 14) Believe the economy's failed dot.coms provide a cautionary lesson for higher education | 713 | 3.19 | 3.20 | 3.17 | .646$n$ |
| 15) Always use social and athletic functions as opportunities to promote my institution | 713 | 4.02 | 4.04 | 3.99 | .431$n$ |
| 16) Accept losses gracefully | 713 | 3.57 | 3.52 | 3.62 | .090$e$ |
| 17) Maintain a measure of mystique | 713 | 3.14 | 3.15 | 3.13 | .837$n$ |
| 18) Am more likely than most presidents to consider alternative methods of delivering higher education | 713 | 3.58 | 3.64 | 3.51 | .031$n$ |
| 19) Choose another CEO as a confidant | 713 | 3.43 | 3.45 | 3.41 | .586$n$ |
| 20) Am highly involved in the community | 713 | 4.30 | 4.39 | 4.20 | .010$n$ |
| 21) Always appear energetic | 713 | 4.35 | 4.43 | 4.27 | .021$n$ |
| 22) Am often viewed as a loner | 713 | 2.52 | 2.51 | 2.54 | .646$n$ |
| 23) Count committee meetings as mistakes | 713 | 2.09 | 2.13 | 2.04 | .118$e$ |
| 24) Would rather be viewed as a strong leader than as a good colleague | 713 | 3.49 | 3.51 | 3.46 | .431$n$ |
| 25) Tend to work long hours | 713 | 4.37 | 4.40 | 4.33 | .205$n$ |
| 26) Often like people who are different | 713 | 4.03 | 4.07 | 3.98 | .107$e$ |
| 27) Only occasionally speak spontaneously | 713 | 2.29 | 2.24 | 2.34 | .090$n$ |
| 28) Participate actively in national higher education organizations | 713 | 3.50 | 3.75 | 3.23 | .000$e$ |
| 29) Dress well | 713 | 4.25 | 4.27 | 4.23 | .586$n$ |
| 30) Care deeply about the welfare of the individual | 713 | 4.53 | 4.53 | 4.54 | .916$n$ |
| 31) Put my institution before myself | 713 | 4.25 | 4.29 | 4.21 | .162$n$ |

(continued)

Table 4.1
(Continued)

| | | | | | |
|---|---|---|---|---|---|
| 32) Encourage creative individuals even though we may disagree | 713 | 4.42 | 4.43 | 4.39 | .586n |
| 33) Appear to make decisions easily | 713 | 3.94 | 4.00 | 3.87 | .042e |
| 34) Appear confident even when in doubt | 713 | 3.99 | 4.01 | 3.96 | .432n |
| 35) Have made decisions that could have resulted in my losing my job if the results had turned out badly | 713 | 4.01 | 4.05 | 3.97 | .162n |
| 36) Am often seen as somewhat aloof | 713 | 2.60 | 2.55 | 2.65 | .090n |
| 37) Enjoy stirring things up | 713 | 3.12 | 3.14 | 3.11 | .646n |
| 38) Am rarely viewed as flamboyant | 713 | 3.69 | 3.65 | 3.73 | .162n |
| 39) Am feared by some | 713 | 3.30 | 3.30 | 3.31 | .916n |
| 40) Smile a lot | 713 | 4.19 | 4.22 | 4.15 | .205n |
| 41) Believe fund-raising and development are my highest priority | 713 | 3.27 | 3.32 | 3.21 | .058n |
| 42) Would consider moving to a better position | 713 | 2.80 | 2.73 | 2.89 | .021n |
| 43) Am viewed as politically adept | 713 | 4.14 | 4.22 | 4.05 | .019n |
| 44) Am viewed by faculty as a strongly academic person | 713 | 3.66 | 3.61 | 3.71 | .090e |
| 45) View the faculty senate as a substantially useless appendage | 713 | 2.21 | 2.19 | 2.23 | .586n |
| 46) Have the strong support of my governing board | 713 | 4.59 | 4.67 | 4.52 | .025e |
| 47) Have successfully concluded many partnerships involving business and government with my institutions | 713 | 3.94 | 4.15 | 3.72 | .000e |
| 48) Make many mistakes | 713 | 2.64 | 2.58 | 2.71 | .031n |
| 49) Am burdened by a governing board that attempts to micromanage the institution | 713 | 1.80 | 1.71 | 1.90 | .010n |

(continued)

Table 4.1
(Continued)

| | | | | | |
|---|---|---|---|---|---|
| 50) Am solely responsible for teaching a course at least once every two years | 713 | 2.29 | 2.16 | 2.44 | .000$e$ |
| 51) Generate many innovative ideas | 713 | 4.19 | 4.28 | 4.08 | .000$e$ |
| 52) Believe the President is the final authority under the governing board | 713 | 4.19 | 4.22 | 4.16 | .287$n$ |
| 53) Believe faculty should make academic decisions | 713 | 3.94 | 3.98 | 3.89 | .118$n$ |
| 54) Am warm and affable | 713 | 4.03 | 4.08 | 3.89 | .118$n$ |
| 55) Believe intercollegiate athletics are in need of reform | 713 | 3.83 | 3.87 | 3.79 | .162$n$ |
| 56) Spend a great deal of time dealing with the media and the press | 713 | 2.96 | 3.05 | 2.87 | .016$n$ |
| 57) Frequently walk my campus and am seen by students and faculty | 713 | 4.16 | 4.14 | 4.18 | .586$n$ |
| 58) Am viewed by minorities and women as highly supportive of them | 713 | 4.21 | 4.22 | 4.19 | .646$e$ |
| 59) Am an internationalist in outlook | 713 | 3.98 | 4.10 | 3.86 | .000$e$ |
| 60) Believe the campus involvement of my spouse or significant other is important | 588 | 3.59 | 3.65 | 3.51 | .045$n$ |
| **Presidential Technology Behavior** | | | | | |
| Use the Internet frequently | 614 | 86.1% | 84.6% | 87.7% | .000$c$ |
| Use a computer frequently | 647 | 90.7% | 88.1% | 93.6% | .000$c$ |
| Carry a cell phone with me when I'm away from the campus | 617 | 86.5% | 86.2% | 86.8% | .383$c$ |
| Require individuals reporting to me to carry a cell phone or pager so they can be reached | 246 | 34.5% | 36.1% | 32.7% | .000$c$ |
| **Presidential Institutions** | | | | | |
| Public Institutions | 372 | 52.2% | 54.1% | 50.0% | .000$c$ |
| Independent Institutions | 341 | 47.8% | 45.9% | 50.0% | .000$c$ |
| Two-Year Institutions | 265 | 37.2% | 31.3% | 43.6% | .000$c$ |

(continued)

Table 4.1
(Continued)

| | | | | | |
|---|---|---|---|---|---|
| Four-Year Institutions | 421 | 59.0% | 65.5% | 52.0% | .000c |
| Other Institutions | 27 | 3.8% | 3.2% | 4.4% | SSI |
| Carnegie Classification | | | | | |
|   1: Doctoral Research Extensive | 47 | 6.6% | 11.1% | 1.8% | .000c |
|   2: Doctoral Research Intensive | 25 | 3.5% | 5.7% | 1.2% | SSI |
|   3: Master's I | 134 | 18.8% | 21.0% | 16.4% | .000c |
|   4: Master's II | 31 | 4.3% | 4.9% | 3.8% | .032c |
|   5: Baccalaureate Liberal Arts | 56 | 7.9% | 10.2% | 5.3% | .000c |
|   6: Baccalaureate General | 68 | 9.5% | 10.2% | 8.8% | .014c |
|   7: Baccalaureate/Associate | 7 | 1.0% | 0.5% | 1.5% | SSI |
|   8: Associate | 265 | 37.2% | 32.6% | 42.1% | .000c |
|   9: Specialized | 67 | 9.4% | 3.8% | 15.5% | .000c |
|   Not Classified | 13 | 1.8% | 0.0% | 3.8% | SSI |
| Year Founded | 690 | 1919 | 1909 | 1930 | .000e |
| Headcount Enrollment, 2001 | 689 | 5968 | 7770 | 3962 | .000e |
| Headcount Enrollment, 1995 | 182 | 9718 | 11686 | 4906 | .000e |
| Annual Budget (000s), 2001 | 220 | $184037 | $226476 | $191164 | .000e |
| Annual Budget (000s), 1995 | 182 | $157041 | $188882 | $79543 | .000e |
| Coeducational | 701 | 96% | 97% | 95% | .024c |
| Tuition and Fees, 2001 | 689 | $8060 | $8096 | $8020 | .790n |
| Freshmen Applications | | | | | |
|   Accepted, 2001 | 307 | 73% | 72% | 74% | .203e |
| SAT Verbal Midrange, 2001 | 247 | 546 | 553 | 532 | .018n |
| ACT Midrange, 2001 | 252 | 22.6 | 22.9 | 22.0 | .023n |
| Freshman with | | | | | |
|   GPA $\geq$ 3.00, 2001 | 179 | 71% | 71% | 73% | .380n |
| Freshmen in Top 10% | | | | | |
|   of HS Class, 2001 | 262 | 40% | 66% | 20% | .000n |
| Freshmen Retention, | | | | | |
|   2001 | 278 | 75% | 77% | 72% | .004e |
| Freshman from Out of State | 306 | 28% | 31% | 25% | .003e |
| Freshmen Minorities | 302 | 21% | 21% | 20% | .571n |
| Freshmen $\geq$ 25 Years | 159 | 7% | 5% | 9% | .077n |
| Undergraduate Women, 2001 | 328 | 58% | 59% | 57% | .293n |
| Classes $\leq$ 20, 2001 | 321 | 55% | 53% | 58% | .017n |
| Student-Faculty Ratio, 2001 | 247 | 15 | 15 | 16 | .518e |
| Full-Time Faculty, 2001 | 328 | 82% | 83% | 80% | .096n |
| Six-Year Graduation Rate, 2002 | 330 | 52% | 53% | 50% | .091n |
| U.S. News Peer Rating, 2001 | 337 | 2.86 | 2.90 | 2.76 | .026e |
| Endowment (000s), 2001 | 224 | $24982 | $30279 | $13800 | .000e |
| Endowment (000s), 1995 | 185 | $12608 | $15967 | $49566 | .000e |
| Gifts Received (000s), 2001 | 224 | $2660 | $3301 | $1306 | .883e |
| Gifts Received (000s), 1995 | 187 | $1433 | $1802 | $546 | .000e |
| Alumni Making Gifts, 2001 | 221 | 18% | 18% | 17% | .710n |

(continued)

Table 4.1
(Continued)

| | | | | | |
|---|---|---|---|---|---|
| Alumni Making Gifts, 1995 | 187 | 22% | 20% | 25% | .002$n$ |
| Gifts Coming from<br>Top 12 Donors, 2001 | 224 | 44% | 42% | 48% | .013$n$ |
| Gifts Coming from<br>Top 12 Donors, 1995 | 187 | 42% | 41% | 42% | .789$n$ |

*For all variables that have a variance (for example, the Likert scale response of a president to the statement "I believe in organizational structure"), a difference of means test was performed in which the mean response of effective presidents was compared to representative presidents. The final column of the table indicates the level of statistical significance attached to the test of the null hypothesis, namely, that there is no difference in the mean response of the two groups.

When one performs such a test, one must assume either that the variances of the two means are equal or that they are unequal. The conventional way to make this determination is to perform a Levene test. This has been done in every case. Unequal variances were assumed unless the null hypothesis of the Levene test, namely, that the variances were equal, was statistically significant at the .10 level or better. The $e$ or $n$ that is reported after the statistical significance indicates whether equal variances ($e$) or unequal variances ($n$) have been assumed.

For all variables that do not have a variance (for example, the percent of presidents who state they are female), a conventional t-test of statistical significance is not possible. Instead, a chi-square test was performed in which the percent of presidents recording this response was compared to the percent of individuals exhibiting the same characteristic in the entire population of presidents. The $c$ that is reported after the level of statistical significance indicates that the chi-square test has been performed.

When SSI appears, it signifies "sample size insufficient" and means that the number of presidents in this portion of the sample was not sufficient to perform a reliable test of statistical significance.

to the institutions where the presidents toil. Our interest in presenting these data is dual. First, we want to provide the reader with a thorough understanding of this rich data set. Not infrequently, questions about the legitimacy of statistical methods ultimately relate to the nature of the data set being utilized. Second, we want to make inferential statistical judgments about these data.

## THE NATURE OF OUR STATISTICAL TESTS

All of the response data for the presidents in Table 4.1 are expressed as means (averages). Therefore, our statistical tests focus on the differences between means. Specifically, we examine the differences between the mean responses of effective versus representative presidents.

We perform two different types of statistical tests here.

1. For variables for which a wide spectrum of values is possible and for which, therefore, the variables have a variance, we perform a conven-

tional difference of means test based upon a t-statistic. Examples of such variables are the age of the president, her published annual salary, or her response to a statement such as "In my own estimation, I place a high value on consensus." Slightly less than one-half of the variables we report are of this variety.

This approach assumes normality in the distribution of presidential responses, which is an acceptable assumption when the number of observations is large, as is generally true for our data. In many cases, we have 713 observations, a very large and comfortable number for such a test. Regardless, we do not report any tests of statistical significance where we have fewer than 30 observations. In such cases, the column of the table recording the statistical significance of our test contains the entry SSI for "sample size insufficient."

When one performs a difference of means test of the sort just described, one must assume either that the variances of the two variables are equal or that they are unequal. This has been done in every situation by applying the Levene test. The italicized letters $e$ and $u$ appended to the statistical probabilities in the last column reflect the Levene test. When an $e$ appears, it refers to situations where the differences of means tests have assumed equal variances; a $u$ reveals situations where the variances are assumed to be unequal.[2]

2. For variables that do not have any variance because they are dummy or categorical variables that take the value of 1 if a characteristic is present, but are empty otherwise, it is not possible to undertake the usual difference of means test involving a t-statistic because such variables have no variance. Examples of such variables include the percentage of presidents who are women, the percentage of presidents who live in the western region of the United States, and so forth. In such cases, we perform a chi-square test, which does not require variance within a variable and does not assume normality. Once again, we do not report any results for variables with fewer than 30 observations. A small, italicized $c$ is appended to statistical probabilities generated by this test.

The most important column in Table 4.1 insofar as the statistical tests are concerned is the final column (the one farthest to the right). For example, for the variable age, we test the null hypothesis that there is no statistically significant difference between the ages of effective and representative presidents. Formally, this test may be expressed as:

*Null Hypothesis*

$H_0$: There is no statistically significant difference in the mean ages of effective and representative presidents.

*Alternative Hypothesis*

$H_A$: There is a statistically significant difference in the mean ages of effective and representative presidents.

The probability recorded in the far right column of Table 4.1 indicates the probability that we can reject the null hypothesis ($H_0$). If we reject the null hypothesis, $H_0$, then we accept the alternative hypothesis ($H_A$). This is equivalent to saying that we believe the evidence supports the notion that there is a difference between effective and representative presidents for the characteristic being examined.

Let's consider an example. The second variable described in Table 4.1 is the mean age of the president when he first became a president. We have 667 observations for this variable (that is, 667 presidents replied). The mean age when effective presidents first became a president is 45.46, while it is 47.79 for representative presidents. The difference, 2.33 years, is statistically significant at the .000 level. That is, this outcome is extremely unlikely if there is no difference between the two groups in this variable among all presidents in the country. Indeed, the .000 tells us we can expect such a difference to occur in a sample such as ours in fewer than 1 in 1,000 instances if actually there is no difference between the effective and representative presidents on this characteristic among the entire population of presidents nationally. This strong result leads us to conclude that we should reject the null hypothesis ($H_0$) and instead accept the alternative hypothesis, $H_A$. In the work that follows, we will report such situations by means of a probability statement enclosed in parentheses such as (p = .000) or (p = .069). Respectively, these statements inform the reader that the probability of the first occurrence is less than 1 in 1,000, while the probability of the second occurrence is less than 69 in 1,000.

How strong do our results have to be before we will reject the null hypothesis and accept the alternative hypothesis? That is, how low must the probability expressed in the far-right column be in order for us to conclude that a statistically significant difference exists between effective and representative presidents? It is not customary to treat a result as statistically significant unless the probability is .10 or less. In some legal proceedings, the standard is .05 or less. However, we will leave the decision with respect to what is statistically important up to the reader, for we believe too much stress sometimes is placed upon tests of statistical significance based upon sets of assumptions that, strictly interpreted, are not fulfilled in many instances. The significance levels we report, then, should act as guides to our interpretation of the statistical results rather than as an immutable razor for decision making. It is foolish to refuse to recognize one relationship that exhibits a statistical significance level of .101, while placing great reliance on another that has a statistical significance level of .099. This is particularly true in light of the large number of observations underpinning this study. Thus, if we have 713 observations for a particular variable, and the statistical significance level is, say, .150, then we should pay attention to this relationship, albeit with an appropriate sense of caution.

## AGE AND EXPERIENCE

The mean age of our presidents is 57.18. Effective presidents are approximately one year older than representative presidents, and this relationship is statistically significant (p = .049). This finding is consistent with Fisher, Tack, and Wheeler (1988)—hereafter referred to as FTW—and McFarlin, Crittenden, and Ebbers (1999). But we would not necessarily have found this result in years past. Studies by Ingraham (1968) and Ferrari (1970) revealed an average age of about 53. Cohen and March (1984) reported that the mean age of college presidents in 1900 was only about 44 and that it rose more or less steadily until 1950, when this process reversed itself and the presidential cohort began to become younger.

Our effective presidents are not only older, but also more experienced, having occupied a presidential role 3.2 years longer than representative presidents. They have also occupied their current presidency 2.9 years longer and assumed their first presidency at a younger age (45.46 versus 47.79). All of these relationships are statistically significant (p = .002 or better). Further, all of these results are consistent with FTW. In general, these results suggest that experience counts where presidential performance is concerned. This is hardly a radical notion, but it is a lesson that some governing boards ignore when they evaluate presidential candidates.[3] "I don't think very many governing boards give that much of a thought," observed a state higher education coordinating board official from the Midwest.

For purposes of comparison, our presidents have served 8.1 years in their presidency, compared to 6.6 years for the ACE presidents. ACE did not ask its sample presidents how many years they had been presidents (at all institutions), but the presidents in our sample have been presidents for 10.3 years. Plausibly, more experienced presidents are more likely to reply to a survey that plumbs their attitudes and behavior.

The Association of Governing Boards (1996) and other authorities have advocated that governing boards give increased consideration to presidential candidates who have experience outside higher education. In our sample, 11.6 percent of the individuals (compared to 14.7 percent in the ACE survey) indicated that their prior position was outside higher education. However, it is important to note that the effective presidents in our sample have spent 2.6 years less time outside higher education than the representative presidents (p = .000). This suggests that the time presidents spent outside the peculiar culture of higher education is less productive than some have thought and actually may generate problems. Or it could mean that this time is a neutral and simply makes presidents older and less experienced in higher education before they occupy their presidencies. The leader of a national faculty organization was adamant when he contended to us, "I've seen too many 'business types' fail when they come into higher education. They think they know the territory, but they don't." Against this, the chair of the governing board of a southern institution that did appoint a very successful president from outside higher education lamented that, "Faculty need to open their minds; many of them automatically assume that an 'outside' president is going to be an insensitive dolt who does not understand what they're doing. And, that's just not true."

While we would not make too much of our finding, it should be of at least modest concern to those such as the Association of Governing Boards that advocate colleges appoint more presidents from outside higher education. Perhaps many American colleges and universities need the fresh vantage point and different experience that a nonacademic president might bring to the position, and such individuals might be needed to stir things up. However, it also could be that such individuals do not come to their presidencies with a full appreciation of the occasionally arcane traditions and procedures and the intensely factional behavior of some American campuses. Arguably, this may be especially true if the nonacademic president does not hold an earned doctorate and has not done significant teaching and research (as we shall see later in this chapter).

## GENDER

Despite recent advances by women, the American college presidency remains a predominantly male bastion, even though women now account for 58 percent of all headcount students. Whereas 80.9 percent of the individuals in our presidential sample are men, 83.6 percent of all effective presidents are men. Stated differently, women account for only 16.4 percent of our effective presidents, though they are 19.1 percent of the sample (p = .000).

Why? A male chauvinist might hypothesize that the answer is simple—women are less effective college presidents than men. However, as we will see in subsequent analysis, the typical female president is less experienced than the typical male president and has occupied her presidency for a shorter period of time. Indeed, the proportion of women presidents in higher education rose from 9.5 percent in 1986 to 21.1 percent in 2001, according to the ACE (2002), and hence many women presidents have only recently been appointed. Women also tend to occupy presidencies in smaller, less prestigious institutions. This indicates that it does not appear to be gender per se that is responsible for the less-than-proportionate appearance of women in the category of effective presidents. Instead, it is their demographic characteristics that are responsible for this. As women presidents gain more experience, they will appear in greater numbers in the effective category. And, "as women presidents are appointed to the presidencies of the really large institutions, they'll get more recognition," predicted a regional accrediting body leader. Multiple regression analysis we report in chapter 6 confirms this.

Notwithstanding this prediction, it should be noted that after some decades of scant movement (Ferrari, 1970), the percentage of women presidents almost doubled between 1988 and 2002. FTW reported that 10.1 percent of their presidents were women in 1988; 19.1 percent of our presidents are women, and 21.1 percent of the ACE presidents were women in 2001. This is robust movement even though women presidents tend to cluster in smaller institutions; ACE reported that 41.6 percent of its women presidents were located at institutions with fewer than 2,000 students.

## ETHNIC BACKGROUND

The proportion of minority presidents rose from 8.1 percent in 1986 to 12.8 percent in 2001, according to the ACE. Of our presidents, 11.2 percent are members of a minority group (FTW found only 7 percent in 1988), with African Americans (4.6 percent) and Hispanic Americans (4.2 percent) leading the way. It is notable that African American presidents are generously represented (5.9 percent) in the effective president category, while the reverse is true for Hispanic American presidents (only 2.4 percent). ($p = .000$ for both relationships.)

One could hypothesize that African Americans are especially competent presidents and Hispanic Americans are the opposite, though there is little evidence to support this notion. The number of Hispanic presidents in our sample ($N = 30$) is sufficiently small that we should be rather cautious about reaching any strong conclusions. In chapter 5, we will examine the characteristics of minority presidents in much greater detail.

## CHARACTERISTICS OF THE PRESIDENT'S INSTITUTION

### Public versus Private

Fifty-two and two-tenths percent of the presidents in our sample are located at public institutions, and 54.1 percent of the effective presidents are situated at public institutions ($p = .000$). Thus, the nature of institutional control is a factor to be taken into consideration as we examine the determinants of presidential effectiveness. Notably, the presidents whom we interviewed were split on the issue of whether or not public or independent status was an advantage in terms of presidential recognition and perceived performance. "Being public is a great deal if you're talking about the flagship institution, but not such a good deal if you're talking about the other state institutions," opined a veteran public university president in the west. ACE did not report comparable data.

### Four-Year Versus Two-Year

The typical president in our survey was located at a four-year institution (59.0 percent), with 37.2 percent holding their appointment at a two-year institution and 3.8 percent in other types of institutions. ACE did not report comparable data.

### Carnegie Classification

The Carnegie Commission (2000) classified all American institutions of higher education according to nine categories, ranging from doctoral research extensive to specialized. The largest number of presidents in our sample serve at two-year institutions (37.2 percent), but they are underrepresented in the effective president category (32.6 percent and $p = .000$). On the other hand, doctoral research-intensive institutions are overrepresented (11.1 percent of effective presidents compared to 6.6 percent of all presidents in our sample and $p = .000$).

These disparities suggest that institutional mission and breadth may well have an influence on experts' perceptions of who is a successful president. "It's silly not to agree that an institution's breadth and depth affect how we perceive the presidents of universities," observed the head of an accrediting association, who also observed that many individuals assume that the presidents of doctoral research-intensive institutions must be highly capable, or they would not have been appointed to their positions. Even so, the mediocre performance of some of these presidents suggests that there is less than a perfect correlation between institutional sophistication (as measured by Carnegie) and presidential performance. The ACE did not report data that would enable us to make comparisons.

There is an alternative hypothesis relating to these data that deserves attention. Psychological distance has been found to be related to presidential effectiveness (see Fisher, 1984 and Fisher, Tack, and Wheeler, 1988 for summaries of this evidence). When a president's constituents become too familiar with her, they too easily recognize her deficiencies, and her ability to benefit from the various charismatic aspects of the presidency is diminished. The result is less effective leadership. Ideally, as a former president put it to us, "A president should be known to everyone, but not really known to anyone." It is difficult to develop and maintain distance in a small, intimate liberal arts college.

In the case at hand, institutional breadth and complexity may be highly correlated with leadership distance and serve as proxies for it. If so, then these institutional characteristics may be sources of presidential effectiveness.

## Enrollment

The mean 2001 headcount enrollment of the institutions in our sample was 5,968. A visible disparity exists, however, between effective and representative presidents in this regard. The mean headcount enrollment of the institutions in which the effective presidents preside is 7,770, whereas it is only 3,962 at the institutions led by representative presidents (p = .000). Perhaps size confers advantageous presidential visibility. "The bigger you are, the more attention you receive, for better or worse," asserted the president of a medium-sized southern public institution. This implies that institution size should be a control variable when we undertake multivariate analysis of the determinants of president success, if not because of the visibility factor, then because of the leadership distance that institutional size provides. ACE did not report comparable data.

## Student Characteristics

In general, the institutions where the effective presidents are located tend to be a bit more selective in admissions, to enroll students with slightly higher SAT and ACT scores (p = .024 or better for these), to have higher student retention (p = .004), and to have higher six-year graduation rates (p = .091). A higher percentage of students located at institutions where the president is in the effective category are from another state (p = .003) and less likely to be nontraditional (25 years or older and p = .077). ACE did not report data relating to student characteristics.

These are not necessarily surprising results. Whether they reflect a cause or an effect is not clear. Do successful presidents create these conditions, or do they flock to such situations? One state university president to whom we talked argued strongly that "Lots of years have to pass before a president will have any real effect on student quality." The president of a community college noted that he will never have any impact on the quality of the students who attend his institution because of its open admission character. We will probe these possibilities with our multivariate analysis in chapter 6, recognizing that our sample will be reduced to about one-third of its original size when we incorporate such variables. For example, we have SAT scores for only 34.6 percent of our institutions. Two-year institutions seldom collect SAT data, and presidents from these institutions constitute more than 37 percent of our sample. Thus, the results we have uncovered are intriguing, but they should be viewed with caution, for they apply to only a slice of American higher education.

## Fund-Raising and Development

Effective presidents preside at institutions with endowments that are more than twice as large as those enjoyed by representative presidents (p = .000). The effective presidents' institutions also raise more than twice as much money on an annual basis (p = .000) and boast a slightly larger proportion of alumni who made a gift in the previous year (but p = .710). "The definition of presidential effectiveness these days is very closely related to his ability to raise money and convince major donors to part with their assets," according to the chair of the governing board of an independent-sector liberal arts college.

We should not find these results surprising, but the same questions concerning cause and effect apply as were true for measures of student quality. Is excellent fund-raising a function of presidential excellence, or vice versa? Further, we once again have a censored, partial sample when we examine fund-raising and development. By way of illustration, we have endowment data for only 31.4 percent of our institutions because most two-year institutions and many historically black colleges and universities do not participate in the industry standard, the annual survey of development activities conducted by the Council for Aid to Education.

## RELIGION

In absolute numbers, more presidents in our survey, and more presidents in the effective category, indicate Roman Catholic as their religious preference than any other preference. But relative to the national population, Roman Catholics are underrepresented as presidents, and they are even more underrepresented as effective presidents. Nationally, 24.5 percent of all individuals indicated a Roman Catholic religious preference (Kosmin and Mayer, 2001), but only 21.5 percent of our presidents do the same (p = .001). An even lower 19.9 percent of effective presidents indicate a Roman Catholic preference (p = .000).

However, presidential underrepresentation is even more striking for Baptists, who constitute 16.3 percent of the national population (Kosmin and Mayer, 2001), but only 8.4 percent of the presidents in our sample (p = .000). On the other hand, most mainline Protestant denominations (Methodist, Presbyterian, Lutheran) are overrepresented relative to their frequency in the American population at large. Presbyterians, for example, constitute only 2.7 percent of the population nationally (Kosmin and Mayer, 2001), but they account for 10.5 percent of all presidents in our survey (p = .000).

Presidents indicating a Jewish religious preference are similarly overrepresented in our sample of presidents, while not a single president in our sample of 713 indicated a Muslim religious preference. Fully 21.9 percent of our presidents either have no religious preference or prefer not to record it. Data from the ACE survey suggest that the proportion of individuals with no religious preference has been rising over time, perhaps reflecting the increasingly secular nature of American society and the growing ranks of institutions that have reduced or terminated their religious affiliations. However, the ACE survey did not record specific Protestant religious preferences.

The religious preference of a presidential candidate no doubt was a more important consideration in years past than currently. Bolman (1965), relying upon a sample of 115 new college presidents appointed in the mid-1960s, found that 110 of 115 were Protestants. Religious preference may be given implicit (and possibly illegal) consideration by governing boards when they appoint presidents. A candidate's religious affiliation (or lack thereof) could act in conjunction with characteristics such as a presidential candidate's ethnic background and perceived social class "to enable governing boards to decide which candidate they believe is the 'best fit' for a presidential slot" (the comment of the chair of the governing board of a religiously affiliated liberal arts college). Or, on the other hand, religious preference today may have little or nothing to do with presidential selection, but instead may be a proxy for long-standing individual disparities in educational backgrounds and previous opportunities and experience that really are important. Our data are not sufficiently detailed to enable to us to determine which of these hypotheses is best supported by the data. Nonetheless, it is remarkable that the proportion of Presbyterian presidents in our sample is quadruple that in the general population. What does this represent, and why does it occur?

## EDUCATION

### Doctoral Degree?

Ninety-one and four-tenths percent of our presidents indicate that they hold some type of an earned doctoral degree; 96.5 percent of effective presidents indicated the same ($p = .000$). Only 82 percent of ACE respondents indicated that they had earned some type of doctoral degree. Of those individuals who hold the doctorate, almost 64 percent possess the Ph.D., but 69.8 percent of our effective presidents hold that degree ($p = .000$). The Ed.D. degree is more heavily associated with representative presidents ($p = .000$), which could reflect either actual performance or the prejudices of conventional arts and science degree holders against those whose degrees are in education.

Six and one-half percent of all presidents in our sample, but only 5.3 percent of effective presidents, hold Law degrees ($p = .000$). Presidents holding the M.D. degree are comparatively rare, with only less than 1 percent of all respondents in our sample falling into that category. The ACE survey data confirm these relationships.

Despite the fact that "Ed.D. degrees are in some sense out of style" (the comment of the leader of a national higher education association) with many presidents and perhaps as well with search firms and governing boards, the earning of a doctorate in education (but being awarded a Ph.D.) is not. Thirty-eight and nine-tenths percent of the presidents in our sample, but only 34.9 percent of effective presidents ($p = .000$), say their major field of concentration in their doctoral work was in education or educational administration. Fully 43.8 percent of the presidents in the ACE survey indicated that education or higher education was the major focus of their doctoral work ($p = .000$). These data uniformly reveal an increasing tendency for college presidents to have completed their doctoral work in a field related to teacher education or educational administration. Bolman (1965) and Ferrari (1970) both found that only 20 percent of the presidents in their studies had earned their highest graduate degree in education, while Ingraham (1968) found 22 percent of his presidents in that category.

The next most common area of study for our presidents was the humanities, with 20.6 percent of all presidents (21.2 percent in the ACE study when religion and theology are included) and 19.0 percent of effective presidents (p = .000). Less than 2 percent of our presidents earned their degrees in business, engineering, or medicine and the health sciences.

Almost exactly one-half of our presidents (50.1 percent) earned their doctoral degree at a public institution; 52.9 percent of effective presidents did so (p = .000). Table 4.2 summarizes the most common institutional sources of those degrees. Indiana University leads the pack, although it was not among the top 16 in the FTW study, where the University of Michigan was the kingpin. Of the 13 institutions granting five or more doctorates to the presidents in our sample, nine are large public universities. We believe that our differing results reflect the broader nature of our presidential sample, which includes many community college presidents. About 20 years ago, Peck (1983) found that his entrepreneurial presidents most frequently had earned their doctorate from a large public university. Our results provide modest support for this notion.

## Baccalaureate Degree?

Ninety-five percent of all of our presidents, and 96.4 percent of effective presidents, indicate that they hold a baccalaureate degree (p = .000).

Table 4.2
Most Common Institutions Granting Presidential Terminal Degrees

| Name of Institution | Number of Presidents Earning Their Terminal Degree |
|---|---|
| Indiana University | 11 |
| Michigan State University | 9 |
| Harvard University | 9 |
| University of Alabama | 8 |
| Northwestern University | 8 |
| University of Michigan | 6 |
| University of Virginia | 6 |
| Purdue University | 5 |
| Pennsylvania State University | 5 |
| Northern Illinois University | 5 |
| University of Southern California | 5 |
| University of Wisconsin | 5 |
| Columbia University | 5 |

It's not clear what the educational status is for the remaining 5 percent of presidents who do not hold a baccalaureate degree. As Table 4.3 reveals, a majority of all presidents in the sample (54.8 percent) earned their baccalaureate degree at a public institution, though 56.7 percent of effective presidents did so (p = .000). However, this must be weighed in light of the reality that 76.5 percent of all college students attended public institutions in 1999 (U.S. Census Bureau, 2003b). Thus, a public college undergraduate pedigree is not the royal road to a college presidency.

Of the 532 presidents who indicated the specific source of their baccalaureate degree, the largest number (35.9 percent) earned their degree from an independent (private) liberal arts college, while almost 10 percent earned their baccalaureate degree from an Ivy League institution or an independent research university. Table 4.3 summarizes these data, which are generally consistent with FTW, though they exhibit a slightly lessened influence of independent institutions as the source of presidential baccalaureate education.

Historically, independent liberal arts colleges have acted as a fertile source for future college presidents. The nation's elite, as least measured by household income and educational levels, frequently sent their children to liberal arts colleges. Gradually, over time, this relationship has eroded, although Table 4.3 discloses that it has hardly disappeared. Graduation from a prestigious liberal arts college still constitutes a highly advantageous credential for those seeking admission to prestigious graduate schools or professional programs. The quality of education remains high in most cases,

Table 4.3
Presidential Baccalaureate Degrees: Institutional Types

| Type of Institution | Number and Percent of Presidents |
|---|---|
| Liberal Arts College | 191 (35.9%) |
| Flagship Public University | 103 (19.4%) |
| Other Public Institution | 132 (24.8%) |
| Ivy League or Seven Sisters | 21 (3.9%) |
| Private Research University | 32 (6.0%) |
| Historically Black College or University | 9 (1.7%) |
| Other | 44 (8.3%) |

and the social and professional contacts students acquire are invaluable for years into the future. Hence, even though public institutions enroll more than three-quarters of all college students, almost one-half of all college presidents earned their baccalaureate degrees at an independent institution.

A perusal of the credentials of the presidents of the most prestigious colleges and universities in the United States reveals a preponderance of individuals who are products of the nation's selective liberal arts colleges. Harvard and Yale are unlikely to appoint as their presidents individuals who are products of so-called directional state colleges, despite the magnificent job such institutions have done in uplifting the conditions of, and generating social and economic mobility for, tens of thousands of individuals in American society. "That is not the image these elite institutions maintain of themselves and their leadership," averred the president of an independent research university. Our data reveal that however skilled and wise, the unfortunate candidate for the presidency of an elite institution who holds a baccalaureate degree from a relatively anonymous regional state institution might as well save her energy. The probability is very low that she will receive extensive consideration. Only a doctoral degree from an absolutely top-flight graduate school, followed by an extremely distinguished set of career achievements, are likely to enable such a candidate to overcome the stigma of her baccalaureate degree from an undergraduate institution of low prestige.

Even so, the majority of college presidencies available today preside over public institutions. Further, the single most common type of higher education institution today is the two-year, junior or community college, the great majority of which are public. In some cases, Ivy League credentials actually may constitute a liability for individuals who would seek to lead a community college. Does he really understand our situation? search and screen committees are bound to inquire. On the other hand, many public universities portray great interest in presidential candidates who hold graduate degrees from prestigious institutions and who are members of Phi Beta Kappa.

Thus, the relationship between institutional control, presidential appointments, and presidential success is a bit murky and idiosyncratic, whether one focuses upon the perceived performance of sitting presidents or upon the path one should take if one aspires to become a president. Higher education is not yet a frictionless enterprise in which the mobility of individuals among institutions is free and easy, regardless of their abilities and qualifications. The nature of one's academic pedigrees and the specific type of degree one has earned still may make a significant difference in how one is perceived and what opportunities one may pursue. The data presented in Table 4.1 and supplied in our surveys support this view.

## The Influence of Specific Coursework

It is generally agreed that the demands upon American college presidents have increased dramatically since World War II. Dozens of books, many of which have been cited in this study, have been written about this phenomenon. A mutating college presidency has brought with it mounting presidential involvement in business and technological deliberations and decisions. Today, presidents must make decisions about wi-fi and privatizing residence halls and hopefully act knowledgeable as they do so. Only a small number of college presidents effectively act as the chief academic officer for their institutions, although this was a very common model a century ago, or even 50 years ago.

Faced with the changing nature of the presidency, some governing boards have expressed the desire to appoint individuals who have previous training in areas such as accounting, computer science, economics, and statistics. This provokes an obvious question—does such training make any difference in presidential performance? Not much, according to Table 4.1. Substantial numbers of all presidents (49.6 percent) have taken two or more courses in economics, but only 49.1 percent of effective presidents have done so ($p = .226$). No positive relationship is apparent. The same general conclusion applies to coursework taken by presidents in the areas of accounting, computer science, and statistics. Indeed, the relationship is negative for accounting ($p = .000$) and computer science ($p = .000$) courses. Those presidents who have taken two or more courses in accounting and computer science are less likely to be viewed as effective by our experts.

At the very least, these data discourage the notion that business- and technology-trained college presidents are likely to exhibit more effectiveness because of the evolving nature of the presidential position. We posit that the primary reason this is true is that the most important decisions college presidents make today relate to questions of values. To be sure, accurate and timely data provide valuable background to any presidential decision, but they are unlikely to inform questions about what colleges ultimately should be doing. The most pressing questions today in American colleges relate to matters such as the appropriate division between undergraduate and graduate work, how we should measure student learning, the efficacy of distance learning, the use of faculty time, the viability of faculty tenure, and campus diversity (Koch, 2003). Accounting courses, for example, cannot contribute very much to discussions concerning campus diversity. Thus, we should not be surprised to find that those presidents who have taken coursework in such areas are no better decision makers than presidents without that background. Similarly, we should not be surprised to find that management nostrums such as TQM that rely heavily upon such notions typically have been discarded as failures.

## Honorary Degrees

Not surprisingly, Table 4.1 divulges that effective presidents have received more honorary degrees than representative presidents. Eighteen and three-tenths percent of effective presidents have received an honorary degree (p = .000), while only 9.9 percent of representative presidents have had such an honor conferred upon them. We believe this discrepancy primarily represents an effect of the productive presidencies of the effective presidents, and only in a few cases represents a causal factor. In a few cases, an honorary degree may lead to further fame and recognition; in most cases, however, it represents recognition of past achievements.

## Scholarly Productivity

The preference of faculty for presidents who "understand what we do because they have done it" (the words of a faculty member we interviewed) is long-standing. Faculty typically desire presidents to have done substantive teaching and research and, preferably, have attained tenure as a faculty member. Peck (1983) reported that his entrepreneurial presidents also were published scholars.

Our effective presidents are less likely than representative presidents to have been solely responsible for teaching a course within the past two years and slightly less likely to feel their faculty view them as strongly academic. Against that, however, it is apparent that our effective presidents are more active as publishing scholars. Table 4.4 illustrates the difference (p = .000 for both books and refereed journal articles).

Table 4.4
Published Work of College Presidents

|  | Effective Presidents | Representative Presidents |
|---|---|---|
| Number of Books Published | 1.44 | .97 |
| Number of Refereed Journal Articles Published | 14.37 | 10.75 |

Thus, it appears that effective presidents often act in a scholarly fashion even though they may not believe they are seen in this light and even though they are not active pedagogues in the classroom. Of course, faculty naysayers might devalue some presidential scholarship by arguing that it focuses on administrivia—administrative and leadership issues rather than hard scholarship in areas such as chemistry, engineering, or history. Our survey data do not allow us to determine what kinds of items our presidents are publishing. Even so, it is apparent that effective presidents have active minds and are wont to share their work with others in the marketplace for ideas.

## POLITICS

As noted previously, the presidents in our survey most often are political Democrats (36.7 percent), followed by those of an independent persuasion (31.2 percent) and those who are Republicans (26.0 percent). Contrast this to Bolman's (1965) finding that 41 percent of presidents identified themselves as Democrats, 37 percent as Republicans, and 22 percent as independents. Our results are hardly surprising; many studies have documented the increasingly independent, Democratic, and liberal political leanings of college faculty and administrators (see Horowitz, 2002, for a summary). More head turning, however, is the clear delineation between effective and representative presidents with respect to Republicanism. Only 20.5 percent of our effective presidents identify themselves as Republicans, while 32.2 percent of representative presidents do so (p = .000).

How might one explain this dichotomy? If the Republican Party is the party of conservatism and if effective presidents are entrepreneurial, change-oriented individuals whose leadership often is not conservative (two rather significant ifs), then Republican political leanings may constitute a marker for several critical leadership qualities and attitudes. Presidents reluctant to entertain change or to take risks may gravitate toward the Republican Party. Of course, there are those who argue that the Republican Party today is the party of change, at least in certain economic and social realms—for example, in its advocacy of educational vouchers and privatization. Nonetheless, to the extent that our ifs are satisfied, the entrepreneurial-versus-conservative explanation may have some validity.

Several presidents whom we interviewed told us they decline to make public their political affiliation. "I walk both sides of the street," explained a president of a medium-sized public institution, who said she attends the political functions of both major parties and provides relatively equal financial support to both parties. On occasion, a president's presumed political identification can be helpful and even have something to do with his appointment. In other cases, however, partisan, public political advocacy by a president can be deadly.[4] Thus, 35.3 percent of our effective presidents (but only 26.9 percent of representative presidents) assert that they are political independents (p = .000). The effective presidents may understand better than representative presidents that public political advocacy can be counterproductive.

## GEOGRAPHIC CONSIDERATIONS

We are interested in the geographic origins and locations of our presidents primarily because they enable us to see if some regions of the country are more productive in terms of nurturing and producing college presidents. Consider Table 4.5, which contrasts the regional origins of college presidents (where they were born) with the region in which their presidency is located. It appears that the Northeast and Midwest regions generate many of the presidents who occupy presidencies in the South and West (p = .000 for both). Presumably, this reflects a variety of factors, including the economic dominance of these regions 50 or 60 years ago, and the relative youthfulness of the populations of the West and certain sections of the South, making it less likely on a proportional basis that large cohorts of prospective presidents exist in these regions. It may also be true that some residual sense of educational inferiority or opportunism may have caused the South and West to import presidents from the Northeast and Midwest regions, where large proportions of elite, prestigious colleges and universities exist. Prospectively, one would expect these differentials to dissipate over time, though there is little sign of this relative to the 1988 FTW study.

Table 4.5
Origin Versus Current Location: Where Presidents Come From and Where They Serve

|  | Born in This Region | Currently Serving as a President in This Region |
|---|---|---|
| Northeast | 18.8% | 17.4% |
| Midwest | 25.9% | 26.2% |
| South | 22.9% | 32.8% |
| West | 8.0% | 17.1% |
| Unidentified Or Other | 24.4% | 6.5% |

## FAMILY CHARACTERISTICS

Effective and representative presidents have just about the same number of children (2.2 or 2.3, very close to the zero population growth level), and the age of their youngest child is just about the same (25 or 26 years). Our experience with governing boards is that on occasion some board members put forward a rather casual verbal hypothesis that presidents with large families and young children will not be as effective because of the demands upon their time. The data in Table 4.1 do not provide much sustenance for this view of the world.

One of the most startling results of the FTW study was their finding that about one-third of all presidents in their sample had fathers who had not completed high school. Similarly, about one-quarter of presidents' mothers did not complete high school. This suggested that there was a fairly high level of social mobility among college presidents. Some 15 years later, we find the same phenomenon, although to a reduced extent. Twenty-three and one-tenth percent of our presidents have a father who did not complete high school; 13.8 percent have a mother who did not complete high school. This finding is even more pronounced for effective presidents ($p = .000$ for both). It remains true that well more than one-half of all of our presidents have fathers or mothers whose educations did not go beyond high school. Early in the twenty-first century, then, we can still assert that the typical sitting college president did not grow up in a highly educated, upper-class home. Social mobility may be decreasing in certain ways, but it remains robust in terms of the sources of American college presidents.

## MARITAL STATUS AND RELATED MATTERS

More than 94 percent of our presidents tell us that they have been married at some time, while 5 to 6 percent of them tell us currently they are divorced. As we will see in chapter 6, 17.6 percent of our women presidents say they never have been married ($p = .000$), and 58.6 percent of women presidents say they are currently married (as opposed to 88.4 percent of men presidents; $p = .000$). In their 1988 study, FTW found that a slightly higher percentage of representative presidents than effective presidents were currently married, though McFarlin, Crittenden, and Ebbers (1999) found the opposite in their study of community college presidents. Our results are consistent with FTW, but they are subject to qualifications we outline later.

Smaller percentages of effective presidents have spouses who are employed full-time ($p = .000$) and who do not attend many campus events ($p = .000$). A larger percentage of the spouses of effective presidents contribute uncompensated time to their institutions than is true for representative presidents (p = .000). These are major divergences. Arguably, many presidential spouses contribute significantly to their husband or wife's presidential success and thereby make a difference (Cotton, 2003).[5] Of interest, however, is the fact that the percentage of all presidents whose spouses are employed (full-time or part-time) apparently has declined. FTW reported that about 60 percent of the spouses of their presidents were employed, while only about 48 percent of our spouses are employed. It appears as if the charge of presidential spouses into the labor market has subsided.

Does marital status make a difference in presidential performance? Our data demand a nuanced answer. On the one hand, effective presidents are currently married slightly less often than representative presidents. On the other hand, women presidents, though married much less often than men, are much more likely to have spouses who are employed full-time and who do not attend many campus events. These latter characteristics are disadvantageous, according to our data. In the most typical presidential situation, a male president has a female spouse who, according to one of our presidential interviewees who leads a modestly endowed liberal arts college, "does all kinds of things to make me more effective and frankly gets the hell exploited out of her by the College"). The notion of two for one (hiring a president and his/her spouse as a team) is illegal in most instances[6] and is guaranteed to infuriate many individuals who regarded marital status as irrelevant and questions relating to it as insulting.

However, if the activities (or lack thereof) of presidential spouses do make a difference in presidential performance, then this presents an interesting conundrum to governing boards. If presidents with spouses who undertake a variety of supportive activities are more likely to be successful, and presidents who have spouses who are not employed are also more likely to be successful, then will this lead to boards discriminating against unmarried and/or female presidential candidates?

We will examine several hypotheses related to these matters when we compare men and women presidents in chapter 5. This is a sensitive area in which social change has been and probably will continue to be rapid, though our evidence suggests the extent of social change has not been quite so rapid as some might believe.

## TECHNOLOGY BEHAVIOR

It is almost trite to observe that we live in a technological age. Of interest, therefore, is how extensively college presidents use available technology as they pursue their administrative tasks. Most of our presidents use many different technologies. For example, 86.1 percent say they use the Internet frequently, in contrast to 68 percent of the general population (Pew, 2003). Ninety and seven-tenths percent tell us they use a computer frequently, and 86.5 percent carry a cell phone when they are away from their campuses. However, only 34.5 percent of our presidents require individuals who report to them to carry a cell phone or pager so that the president can reach them.

Of considerable interest, however, are the differences we observe between our effective and representative presidents. In general, our effective presidents are less heavy users of technology than our representative presidents, except in the case in which they require reportees to carry a cell phone or pager, which more effective presidents are inclined to do (p = .000). It appears that effective presidents are concerned that they remain in touch with key colleagues who report to them, but they also do not want to spend exorbitant numbers of hours looking at computer screens (p = .000), so perhaps they use the Internet less intensively than representative presidents (p = .000). "If you spend too much time staring at your microcomputer, you soon get out of touch with your campus, your board and your big givers," warned a president we interviewed. Consensus building, the cultivation of large donors, and vision selling are activities that by and large are not amenable to computer or Internet administrative approaches. It appears that effective presidents may possess a more finely honed understanding of this.

## PRESIDENTIAL ATTITUDES AND VALUES

Before we explore the responses of presidents to 60 distinct statements designed to elicit their attitudes, values, and behavior, a caveat is in order. As was true for the variables we have described in the previous sections, what may appear to be a significant difference between effective and representative presidents on a specific item actually may reflect differing demographics, institutional affiliations, and other factors. In other words, observed differences between the two groups of presidents (or the absence of a difference) in some cases may not represent truly important differences in attitudes, values, and behavior that actually account for their success but instead may simply reflect who they are demographically and the characteristics of their institutions. Thus, once we hold these other relevant factors constant, it is possible that relationships may disappear (or appear). For example, it may not be femaleness, per se, that is responsible for the pairwise differences between men and women presidents that we observe.

Instead, it may be the differing personal characteristics of men and women presidents that are critical. Men presidents, for example, are older and more experienced than women presidents, and such factors make a difference. That is why we will undertake multivariate analysis in chapter 6.

Heavy majorities of all of our presidents say that

Respect from those they lead is crucial.

Effective leaders take risks.

Consensus is important.

Leaders should be perceived as self-confident.

Leaders should serve the people.

They are sometimes viewed as assertive.

They delegate responsibilities to subordinates.

They value one-on-one meetings.

They are highly involved in their communities.

They always appear energetic.

They tend to work long hours.

They dress well.

They care deeply about the welfare of the individual.

They put their institutions before themselves.

They encourage creative individuals.

They smile a lot.

They are politically adept.

They have the strong support of their governing boards.

They generate many innovative ideas.

They believe the president is the final authority under the governing board.

They frequently walk their campuses and are seen.

They are viewed as highly supportive by minorities and women.

On the other hand, our overall sample of presidents is less likely to say they

Are often viewed as loners

Count committee meetings as mistakes

Are often seen as somewhat aloof

View the faculty senate as a substantially useless appendage

Make many mistakes

Are burdened by a governing board that micromanages

Are solely responsible for teaching a course

Yet, several of the most interesting findings in Table 4.1 relate to differences between our effective and representative presidents. Noticeable gaps exist between effective and representative presidents in several areas. For example, a higher proportion of effective than representative presidents say they

Place a high value on consensus (p = .090)
FTW's finding is similar.[7]
Believe they frequently violate the status quo (p = .019)
FTW's findings conflict, but their result falls far short of being statistically significant. This result confirms Peck's (1983) early findings concerning his successful presidents.
Are more likely than most to consider alternative methods of delivering higher education (p = .031)
FTW did not test this hypothesis.
Are highly involved in the community (p = .010)
FTW's finding conflicts, but their result is not statistically significant.
Always appear energetic (p = .021)
FTW's findings are similar.
Participate actively in national higher education organizations (p = .000)
FTW did not test this hypothesis in this form.
Appear to make decisions easily (p = .042)
FTW's findings differ slightly, but they are not statistically significant.
Believe fund-raising and development are their highest priority (p = .058)
FTW did not test this hypothesis.
Believe they are politically adept (p = .019)
FTW did not test this hypothesis.
Believe they have the strong support of their governing board (p = .025)
FTW did not test this hypothesis.
Have concluded many successful partnerships with business and government (p = .000)
FTW did not test this hypothesis.
Believe they generate many innovative ideas (p = .000)
FTW did not test this hypothesis. Peck (1983) found this to be true for his successful presidents.
Spend a great deal of time dealing with the media and the press (p = .016)
FTW did not test this hypothesis.
Are an internationalist in outlook (p = .000)
FTW did not test this hypothesis.

Believe the involvement of their spouse or significant other is important
(p = .045)

FTW did not test this hypothesis.


On the other hand, effective presidents are less likely than representative presidents to say they

Believe in organizational structure (p = .000)

FTW's findings conflict, but this is consistent with Peck's (1983) results.
Peck's successful, entrepreneurial presidents frequently circumvented
their formal organizations, particularly in times of crisis, and they were
less likely to be devotees of extensive institutional strategic planning.

Believe a leader serves the people (p = .090)

FTW's finding conflicts, but it is not statistically significant.

Accept losses gracefully (p = .090)

FTW's finding conflicts, but it was not statistically significant.

Only occasionally speak spontaneously (p = .090)

FTW's findings conflict.

Often are seen as somewhat aloof (p = .090)

FTW's findings are similar, but not statistically significant.

Would consider moving to a better position (p = .021)

FTW did not test this hypothesis.

Are viewed by faculty as a strongly academic person (p = .090)

FTW did not test this hypothesis. Even though effective presidents publish
more than representative presidents, they do not believe their faculty
see them as strongly academic.

Make many mistakes (p = .031)

FTW did not test this hypothesis.

Have a board that micromanages (p = .010)

FTW did not test this hypothesis.

Are solely responsible for teaching a course at least once every two years (p
= .000)

FTW did not test this hypothesis.


In an overall sense, we presented our sample of 713 presidents with 60
statements such as those we have just examined. FTW presented their sample of about 615 presidents with 40 such statements. There is substantial

overlap in 34 of our statements. In only two cases do we find significant disagreement.

> Our effective presidents are much less likely to believe in organizational structure ($p = .090$); FTW's effective presidents were the reverse, and that relationship was statistically significant at the .05 level. Our results, however, are consistent with Peck (1983).

> Our effective presidents are less likely to say that only on occasion do they speak spontaneously; that is, they do speak spontaneously with some frequency ($p = .090$). FTW found the opposite ($p = .0001$).

Not surprisingly, we prefer our results, which are fortified by the multivariate analysis presented in chapter 6. As noted at the beginning of this chapter, bivariate statistical relationships can disappear when tested as a part of a multivariate relationship. We believe that to be the case with respect to the matter of organizational structure, which is an important part of a set of characteristics that relate to entrepreneurial attitudes, values, and behavior.

The question of whether or not presidents should speak spontaneously has always been an interesting one. The very nature of the modern college presidency dictates that presidents cannot avoid circumstances where they must speak spontaneously. FTW argue that successful presidents minimize the number of these situations, which they regard as unpredictable and susceptible to episodes where presidents "shoot off their mouths without thinking" (the comment of a flagship state university president we interviewed). We are reminded of a president who acquired a reputation for being less than thoughtful because he often prematurely revealed major decisions in seemingly unimportant meetings. He soon learned that nothing is off the record when a president speaks.

Even so, it is evident that some presidents perform exceptionally well in a spontaneous milieu and gain both friends and respect when they speak cogently in unrehearsed situations. When done well, such events demonstrate the president's expertise, confidence, and command. They contribute to her charisma and public presence. It is also true that the nature of public speaking opportunities for presidents has changed in recent years. The advent of talk radio, for example, has provided presidents with new opportunities to communicate their vision and present their institutional case. Some presidents thrive in such circumstances and gain the reputation of being open, accessible, candid, and well informed.

Of course, the "ambush tendency of media representatives to act as if they are Mike Wallace" (the pithy observation of a community college president who operates in a delicate ethnic environment) and the joy with which media representatives push a microphone into an unprepared presidential face and ask or stimulate loaded questions has increased over time, and an astute president must be prepared for outrageously unfair questions and innuendos. The same president told us, "If you're not ready to answer a question the equivalent of 'When did you stop beating your wife?', then you shouldn't put yourself in that situation."

Our data indicate that successful presidents often do speak spontaneously and, further, that they have learned to master unpredictable situations. Of course, it is one thing to take spontaneous questions on Parents' Weekend and quite another to submit to the tender mercies of a hostile talk show host with an earned reputation for skewering his guests. The wise president will choose her public speaking opportunities judiciously and always, always come prepared. Presidential effectiveness, our data tell us, can be enhanced by articulate, commanding presidential spontaneity; however, spontaneity is a two-edged sword and may lead some presidents into a swamp of problems.

## SUMMARIZING THE DATA SET

Speaking generally, it is evident that our data set is consistent with the major previous study in the area (Fisher, Tack, and Wheeler, 1988), the more limited McFarlin, Crittenden, and Ebbers (1999) study of community college presidents, and the biannual American Council on Education (2002) demographic studies of the American presidency. This is encouraging, for as we move in succeeding chapters to test additional statistical tests on sets of potentially controversial hypotheses relating to gender, ethnic background, and entrepreneurial behavior, we can be confident that the basis for our work is solid.

# CHAPTER 5

# Gender, Race, and the American College Presidency: Statistical Tests

It doesn't matter if a cat is black or white, so long as it catches mice.
—Deng Xiaoping, former Premier of the People's Republic of China

I'm interested in the fact that the less secure a man is, the more likely he is to have extreme prejudice.
—Clint Eastwood, American actor

Since 1986, the percentage of women college presidents has increased from 9.5 percent to 21.1 percent,[1] while the percentage of minority presidents increased from 8.1 percent to 12.8 percent (ACE, 2002). Whereas the sample FTW took in the mid-1980s contained 62 women and 28 identifiable minority presidents, the changes of the past 15 years generated 136 women and 80 identifiable minority presidents for our sample. This is by itself a statement about the evolution of society and higher education.

The question we address in this chapter is this—How, if at all, do women and minority presidents differ from male and Caucasian presidents in their attitudes, values, and behavior? On occasion, there has been controversy attached to these questions and their answers. For example, some observers argue that women leaders and women college presidents have distinctive modes of thought and operation that clearly differentiate them from men. A representative survey of these views may be found in Chliwniak (1997, 46), who asserts (with reference to leadership styles) that women adopt "a more democratic or participative style, whereas men tended to adopt a more autocratic or directive style." Fisher (1984) and FTW agree that differences may exist between women and men presidents in terms of their leadership styles. Nevertheless, they believe excellent leaders, whatever their styles, ultimately utilize the same tools of power and leadership to move their institutions and accomplish their ends.

A review of the literature in this area reveals that a remarkably large proportion of the empirical evidence is anecdotal rather than comprehensive, frequently impressionistic, and sometimes laced with emotion. Further, of the large-sample empirical evidence that is available, much has been generated by sometimes disputed instruments such as the Myers-Briggs test. In general, there is a paucity of large-sample, statistically rigorous empirical evidence that contrasts the leadership of the genders. Further, relevant to our purposes, there is virtually no rigorous empirical evidence on gender that relates to college presidents. For example, neither FTW nor McFarlin, Crittenden, and Ebbers (1999) distinguished between women and men presidents in most of their statistical results.

Much the same discussion can be applied to minority presidents.[2] There is very little rigorous, replicable statistical evidence available that contrasts minority leaders or college presidents with nonminorities. Are they individuals who utilize the same principles of leadership as majority presidents, albeit with different habits, styles, and operational modes that reflect personal preferences and local custom? We don't know and hence cannot say if minority college presidents constitute a unique group, *sui generis*.

Few would deny that HBCUs (historically Black colleges and universities) such as the University of Maryland—Eastern Shore or Florida Memorial College constitute very different academic and administrative turf than typical majority institutions such as Bowling Green State University or California Lutheran University. The relevant question, nonetheless, is whether ultimately this makes a significant difference. That is one of the topics we attack in this chapter.

## WOMEN PRESIDENTS VIS-À-VIS MEN PRESIDENTS

Table 5.1 presents data that compare and contrast the women and men presidents in our survey group. To make this task manageable, only those differences between women and men that are statistically significant at the .10 level or better are presented.

## GENDER: A CLOSER LOOK AT PERSONAL CHARACTERISTICS

Compared to men presidents, women presidents

Are less likely to hold an earned doctorate

Table 5.1

Gender Differences in Presidential Characteristics, Values, Attitudes, and Activities

**Personal Characteristics and Background**

|  | **Responses of Male Presidents** | **Responses of Female Presidents** |
|---|---|---|
| Hold a doctorate | 85.6% | 82.4% |
| Hold a Ph.D. | 59.6% | 50.7% |
| Hold an Ed.D. | 21.3% | 25.7% |
| Hold honorary degrees | 13.5% | 17.6% |
| Hold an M.Ed. | 14.2% | 17.6% |
| Hold a B.A. | 56.3% | 66.2% |
| Hold a B.S. | 38.6% | 29.4% |
| Have taken two or more courses in statistics | 60.3% | 65.4% |
| Have taken two or more courses in accounting | 22.2% | 17.6% |
| I was a college president previous to this position | 79.4% | 75.0% |
| Age | 57.5 | 55.7 |
| Age upon becoming a president | 46.3 | 47.9 |
| Total years in higher education | 24.0 | 20.9 |
| Total years as a president | 10.8 | 7.8 |
| Years in current presidency | 8.6 | 6.4 |
| Caucasian | 85.3 | 83.8 |
| Number of books published | 1.3 | 0.9 |
| Number of refereed articles Published | 13.2 | 10.3 |
| Number of professional memberships | 5.3 | 6.4 |
| Presidential Salary | $163784 | $152762 |
| Roman Catholic | 19.1% | 31.6% |
| Never married | 2.8% | 17.6% |
| Now married | 88.4% | 58.8% |
| Spouse employed full-time | 29.5% | 41.9% |
| Spouse employed part-time | 18.2% | 7.4% |
| Spouse contributes uncompensated time | 65.2% | 30.1% |
| Spouse does not attend most events | 12.1% | 22.8% |
| Born in the northeast region of the U.S. | 18.0% | 22.1% |
| Reside in the northeast region of the U.S. | 15.9% | 23.5% |
| Reside in the south region of the U.S. | 34.1% | 27.2% |

(continued)

Table 5.1
(Continued)

| | | |
|---|---|---|
| Politically a Democrat | 33.6% | 50.0% |
| Politically a Republican | 28.6% | 15.4% |
| Father's education less than high school | 23.6% | 20.6% |
| Mother's education less than high school | 14.6% | 9.6% |

**Institutional Characteristics**

| | Responses of Male Presidents | Responses of Female Presidents |
|---|---|---|
| Headcount enrollment, 2001 | 6181 | 5078 |
| Public institution | 52.0% | 56.0% |
| Carnegie research institution | 7.2% | 4.5% |
| Two-year Institution | 35.2% | 48.5% |
| Single sex institution | 1.8% | 13.3% |
| Institutional annual budget, 2001 | $199.8m. | $105.8m. |
| U.S. News peer ranking, 2002 | 2.88 | 2.76 |
| Women undergrads, 2001 | 55.6% | 69.7% |
| Frosh applications accepted, 2001 | 72.6% | 74.8% |
| Frosh with HS GPA $\geq$ 3.00, 2001 | 72.4% | 74.8% |
| Frosh out of state, 2001 | 43.1% | 47.5% |
| Frosh who are minorities, 2001 | 19.7% | 26.7% |
| Frosh 25+ years of age, 2001 | 6.3% | 8.1% |
| Mean institutional six-year graduation rate, 2001 | 51.2% | 54.5% |
| Classes under 20 students, 2001 | 53.1% | 63.3% |
| Student/Faculty ratio, 2001 | 15.7 | 13.6 |
| Full-time faculty, 2001 | 82.8% | 78.5% |

**Values, Attitudes and Activities**

| | Responses of Male Presidents | Responses of Female Presidents |
|---|---|---|
| Believe that an effective leader takes risks | 4.68 | 4.79 |
| Place a high value on consensus | 3.94 | 4.10 |
| Believe in merit pay | 4.01 | 3.89 |
| Am sometimes viewed as assertive | 4.16 | 4.30 |
| Delegate responsibility and authority to subordinates | 4.57 | 4.47 |
| Believe in the value of one on one meetings | 4.51 | 4.40 |
| Maintain a measure of mystique | 3.20 | 2.89 |
| Choose another CEO as a confidant | 3.38 | 3.65 |
| Always appear energetic | 4.32 | 4.49 |
| Am often viewed as a loner | 2.56 | 2.39 |
| Would rather be viewed as a strong leader than as a good colleague | 3.56 | 3.18 |

(continued)

Table 5.1
(Continued)

| | | |
|---|---|---|
| Tend to work long hours | 4.35 | 4.45 |
| Often like people who are different | 3.99 | 4.18 |
| Participate actively in national higher education organizations | 3.44 | 3.79 |
| Am often seen as somewhat aloof | 2.63 | 2.47 |
| Am rarely viewed as flamboyant | 3.72 | 3.54 |
| Smile a lot | 4.14 | 4.40 |
| Am viewed by faculty as a strongly academic person | 3.63 | 3.79 |
| View the faculty senate as a substantially useless appendage | 2.23 | 2.12 |
| Have the strong support of my governing board | 4.62 | 4.51 |
| Am burdened by a governing board that attempts to micromanage the institution | 1.78 | 1.88 |
| Am solely responsible for teaching a course at least once every two years | 2.38 | 1.95 |
| Believe the President is the final authority under the governing board on all matters affecting the institution | 4.26 | 3.91 |
| Am warm and affable | 3.99 | 4.19 |
| Spend a great deal of time dealing with the media and the press | 3.00 | 2.78 |
| Am viewed by minorities and women as highly supportive of them | 4.16 | 4.43 |
| Believe the campus involvement of my spouse or significant other is important | 3.74 | 2.96 |

Note: Only those characteristics are presented in which: (1) there is a statistically significant difference at the .10 level or better in the responses of men and women, with statistical significance determined either by a difference of means test or a chi-square test, as outlined in Table 4.1; (2) sample size was sufficient to draw a meaningful inference. Statistical significance and sample size are related.

Are less likely to have earned a Ph.D. and more likely to have earned an Ed.D.

Are more likely to have earned an honorary degree

Are more likely to have earned a B.A. degree and less likely to have earned a B.S. degree

Are more likely to have taken two or more courses in statistics, but less likely to have taken two or more courses in accounting

Are less likely to have been a president once before

Are 1.8 years younger

Were 1.6 years older when they were appointed to their first presidency

Have been in higher education 3.1 fewer years

Have spent 3.0 fewer years as a president

Have been in their current presidency 2.2 fewer years

Are less likely to be Caucasian

Have published fewer books and refereed scholarly articles

Hold more memberships in professional organizations

Earn more than $11,000 less as a president on an annual basis

Are more than 50 percent more likely to be Roman Catholic

Are five times more likely to never have been married

Are one-third less likely to be married currently

Are one-third more likely to have a spouse who is employed full-time

Are about one-half as likely to have a spouse who is employed part-time

Are less than one-half as likely to have a spouse who contributes significant uncompensated time to the president's institution

Are almost twice as likely to have a spouse who does not attend most college events

Are more likely to have been born in, and reside in, the northeast region of the United States and less likely to reside in the south region of the United States

Are about 50 percent more likely to be a political Democrat and almost 50 percent less likely to be a political Republican

Are less likely to have either a father or a mother who did not complete high school

Are more likely to use the Internet frequently

Are more likely to use a computer frequently

Are more likely to carry a cell phone with them when they are away from campus

Are more likely to require their most important reportees to carry a cell phone with them when those individuals are away from campus

It is important to note, however, that the differences cited tend to diminish if one examines more homogenous groups of women and men presidents. For example, if one focuses only on effective presidents, then the observed differences between women and men presidents tend to be smaller than they are when one examines all presidents. That is, effective women presidents tend to resemble effective men presidents more than all women presidents resemble all men presidents. The attributes that produce presidential effectiveness are not quite as variable, women versus men, as some observers have theorized. Attributes that produce effective women presidents are similar to those that produce effective men presidents.

## GENDER: A CLOSER LOOK AT INSTITUTIONAL CHARACTERISTICS

Compared to the institutions in which men presidents hold sway, the institutions where women are presidents

Are about 1,100 students smaller in headcount

Are more likely to be public

Are less likely to be a Carnegie research extensive institution

Are more than one-third more likely to be a two-year institution

Are more than seven times as likely to be a single-sex institution

Have annual budgets that are only a bit more than one-half the size

Have slightly lower peer ratings in the annual *U.S. News and World Report* survey

Have about one-quarter more women students as a proportion of the total student body

Are slightly less selective in freshmen admissions

Have slightly more out-of-state students

Have about two-fifths more minority students as a proportion of the total student body

Have about two-fifths more nontraditional students age 25 or more

Have higher institutional six-year graduation rates

Offer about one-quarter more classes enrolling less than 20 students

Have lower student/faculty ratios

Have a lower percent of full-time faculty

## GENDER: A CLOSER LOOK AT ATTITUDES, VALUES, AND ACTIVITIES

Compared to men presidents, women presidents tell us they are

More likely to support the idea that an effective leader takes risks

More likely to place a high value on consensus

Less likely to believe in merit pay

More likely to be viewed as assertive

Less likely to delegate responsibilities

Less likely to believe in the value of one-on-one meetings

Less likely to believe they maintain a level of mystique

More likely to choose another CEO as a confidant

More likely to appear energetic

Less likely to be perceived as a loner

Less likely to prefer to be viewed as a strong leader rather than as a good colleague

More likely to work long hours

More likely to like individuals who are different

More likely to participate actively in national higher education organizations

Less likely to be viewed as aloof

More likely to be viewed as flamboyant

More likely to smile a lot

More likely to believe they are viewed by faculty as a strong academic person

Less likely to view the faculty senate as a substantially useless appendage

Less likely to have the strong support of their governing board

More likely to have a governing board that micromanages

Less likely to be solely responsible for teaching a course at least once every two years

Less likely to subscribe to the view that the president is the final authority under the governing board for all matters affecting the institution

More likely to be viewed as warm and affable

Less likely to spend a great deal of time dealing with the media and the press

More likely to believe they are viewed as highly supportive of women and minorities

Less likely to believe the involvement of their spouse or significant other is important

## GENDER: DRAWING CONCLUSIONS

In chapter 4, we saw that women presidents were less likely than men presidents to appear in the effective president group (p = .000). We hypothesized that this was due to differences in background and experience. In fact,

Table 5.1 demonstrates that women presidents as a group are less likely to hold a doctorate, are younger, have spent less time in higher education, have been a president for fewer years, and have been in their current presidency fewer years. All of these results are highly significant in a statistical sense. Further, women presidents have published fewer books and refereed journal articles. It seems plausible that these differences worked to the disadvantage of women when our experts nominated individual presidents as especially successful and effective. Hence, our results should not be surprising.[3]

Women presidents also tend to be located at smaller, less research-intensive institutions with smaller annual budgets, and they more frequently hold their presidency at a two-year college. The institutions led by women presidents (relative to men) tend to be somewhat less selective in terms of admissions and to receive slightly lower peer ratings in *U.S. News and World Report's* annual survey. Their students drop out at a slightly higher rate and graduate at a slightly higher rate than the students at institutions with men presidents. Both class sizes and student/faculty ratios are lower at the colleges where women are presidents.[4]

Further, as we already discovered in chapter 4, the marital status of women presidents as a group is different from that of men. Whether or not one approves of the circumstances that lead to the following conditions, it is nonetheless true that noticeably more effective presidents than representative presidents have spouses or significant others who contribute considerable uncompensated time to their institutions. Further, the spouses or significant others of effective presidents are much less likely to work full-time than those connected to representative presidents.

It is clear from our data that these also are areas where women presidents differ significantly from men—and apparently to their disadvantage. As noted earlier in this chapter, women presidents, relative to men, are much less likely to be currently married and much less likely to have spouses or significant others who contribute considerable uncompensated time to the president's institution. In addition, the spouses or significant others of women presidents are much more likely to work full-time. Not being married, per se, may not be a disadvantage, but what one's spouse does if one is married does appear to make a difference.

Thus, our results suggest that active, participating spouses are a plus for a president and that presidents without such spouses operate at a perceptual disadvantage, regardless of whatever rhetoric may be dispensed in public by governing boards and presidents. We do not argue that this is *always* true; we do assert that our evidence indicates it *frequently* is true. We understand fully that many individuals may regard the facts we discovered as depicting an inequitable situation, but equity often has little relation to reality.

The views of those who contend that women administrators behave in a different fashion than men draw mixed support from our results. Women presidents place a higher value on consensus than men presidents, are more supportive of faculty senates, believe they more often like individuals who are different, believe they are less likely to be viewed as aloof, believe that they are more likely to be viewed as warm and affable, and report that they smile more. These personality traits are generally supportive of the humane characteristics that Chliwniak (1997), drawing on the work of authors such as Milwid (1990), Helgesen (1990, 1995), Kelly (1991), West and Zimmerman (1991), and Naisbitt and Auberdene (1992) broadly attributed to women academic leaders.

On the other hand, more women presidents than men believe they are viewed as assertive, and women presidents more often see themselves as flamboyant. Further, they are less likely than men presidents to believe one-on-one meetings are productive and similarly are less likely to delegate their responsibilities. Many would regard these characteristics as less consistent with, or even inconsistent with, what a woman president we interviewed labeled the "caring, sharing" scenario.

At the same time, women presidents are much less likely than men to believe that the involvement of their spouse or significant other is important. They are more likely to have a governing board they believe micromanages them, but they are less likely to believe that they have the strong support of that board. None of these would be seen as a positive by most observers.

Of interest is that women presidents are considerably less likely than men presidents to subscribe to the view that they hold the final authority under their governing board for all matters affecting the institution. Supporters of the notion that women presidents are more humane and collegial than men likely would nod in approval of this finding. However, such an attitude about the nature of final campus authority not only is legally suspect, but it also may constitute a recipe for problems if it results in indecision and reluctance to take responsibility. Campuses that drift because no one will exercise authority or accept responsibility ordinarily are neither entrepreneurial nor successful.

One area where the behavior of women and men presidents clearly differs is in terms of the extent to which they rely upon modern technology in their administrative routines. By usual societal standards, virtually every college president today is a heavy user of technology; however, this is especially true for women. Women presidents report that they use both the Internet and computers more than men presidents, and they are more heavily dependent upon cell phones to conduct their business. Further, they are more likely to use technology to maintain contact with the major administrators who report to them. These are behaviors that, all things considered, may be disadvantageous to women presidents, at least based upon our evidence.

The bivariate results we reported in chapter 4 suggest that effective presidents are on the whole less intensive users of modern technology than representative presidents. It is difficult to "grip and grin" (the intriguing phraseology of a president of a military-related institution to describe his intensive handshaking and group socializing) if one is ensconced in front of a computer screen. If women are indeed more attached to certain forms of technology than men, then this might account for another of our findings, namely, that women presidents have a reduced preference for one-on-one meetings, compared to men presidents. Query whether such preferences and behavior are supportive of the democratic, participative, caring, sharing hypothesis that some argue is empirically valid for women administrators; probably not.

## MINORITY PRESIDENTS VIS-À-VIS CAUCASIAN PRESIDENTS

As Fisher and Koch (1996, 91) have pointed out, "Most of the discussion of the managerial styles of African-American managers and college presidents is impressionistic and anecdotal." Things have not changed dramatically. Virtually the same statement might still be put forward in 2003 concerning what we actually know about all minority managers and minority college presidents. There is little broad, rigorously obtained evidence describing the attitudes, values, and behavior of minority leaders and college presidents. Exemplary is the study of Posner and Kouzes (1993) who examined a sample of 35,000 employees and managers but found no substantive differences in the management *practices* of minority managers vis-à-vis Caucasian managers. There is evidence, however, that the *styles* of minority managers differ from those of Caucasian managers (Morrison and Van Glinow, 1990, provide evidence).

Hence, we can make very few credible generalizations about the attitudes, values, and especially the behavior of minority college presidents because there is a dearth of rigorous, replicable, large-sample statistical work on the subject. The evidence that is available tends to concentrate upon African Americans rather than Asian Americans or Hispanic Americans. This is a joint function of history and small sample sizes.

Yet it is also true that much of the evidence available concerning minority college presidents is anecdotal and sometimes hagiographic. Consequently, while these contributions are the basis for many interesting

Table 5.2
Ethnic Differences in Presidential Characteristics, Values, Attitudes, and Activities

<u>**Personal Characteristics and Background**</u>

| | Responses of Caucasian Presidents | Responses of Minority Presidents |
|---|---|---|
| Baccalaureate degree | 95.0% | 92.4% |
| Baccalaureate degree from public institution | 49.6% | 59.5% |
| I was a college president previous to this position | 77.4% | 75.9% |
| Number of books published | 1.16 | 0.9 |
| Number of refereed articles Published | 12.6 | 11.6 |
| Number of professional memberships | 5.4 | 6.3 |
| I have held office in my most important national organization | 48.0% | 51.9% |
| Roman Catholic | 21.8% | 30.4% |
| Politically a Democrat | 37.5% | 41.8% |
| Politically a Republican | 26.5% | 12.7% |
| Now married | 83.4% | 86.0% |
| Spouse employed full-time | 32.8% | 36.7% |
| I use the Internet frequently | 87.7% | 91.1% |
| I use a computer frequently | 92.3% | 94.4% |
| I carry a cell phone with me when I'm away from campus | 86.8% | 91.1% |
| I require the most important individuals who report to me to carry a cell phone or pager so I can reach them | 34.2% | 44.3% |
| Father's education less than high school | 23.0% | 32.9% |
| Mother's education less than high school | 13.7% | 24.0% |

<u>**Institutional Characteristics**</u>

| | Responses of Caucasian Presidents | Responses of Minority Presidents |
|---|---|---|
| Headcount enrollment, 2001 | 5413 | 6041 |
| Public institution | 54.0% | 62.8% |
| Institutional annual budget, 2001 | 199.8m. | $105.8m. |
| U.S. News peer ranking, 2002 | 2.85 | 2.68 |
| Frosh applicants accepted, 2001 | 72.3% | 69.1% |

(continued)

Table 5.2
(Continued)

| | | |
|---|---|---|
| ACT midrange, 2001 | 22.4 | 19.3 |
| Frosh with high school GPA ≥ 3.00, 2001 | 69.7% | 51.7% |
| Frosh in top 10% of high school class, 2001 | 43.0% | 38.8% |
| Frosh retention, 2001 | 74.8% | 71.2% |
| Frosh 25+ years of age | 7.1% | 10.9% |
| Mean institutional six-year graduation rate, 2001 | 51.1% | 40.7% |
| Classes sizes under 20 students, 2001 | 55.1% | 51.5% |
| Full-time faculty, 2001 | 81.8% | 79.7% |
| Annual fund raising, 2001 | $12.8m | $8.4m. |
| Alumni who gave a gift, 2001 | 17.6% | 11.1% |
| Endowment, 2001 | $248.1m. | $45.0m. |

**Values, Attitudes and Activities**

| | Responses of Caucasian Presidents | Responses of Minority Presidents |
|---|---|---|
| Am sometimes viewed as hard nosed | 3.59 | 3.80 |
| Believe in organizational structure | 4.12 | 4.28 |
| Believe in close collegial relationships with faculty | 3.85 | 4.01 |
| Believe in merit pay | 3.98 | 4.20 |
| Am sometimes viewed as assertive | 4.18 | 4.41 |
| Frequently violate the status quo | 3.84 | 3.72 |
| Always use social and athletic functions as opportunities to promote my institution | 4.00 | 4.10 |
| Maintain a measure of mystique | 3.14 | 3.53 |
| Am more likely than most presidents to consider alternative methods of delivering higher education | 3.55 | 3.67 |
| Choose another CEO as a confidant | 3.40 | 3.57 |
| Count committee meetings as mistakes | 2.07 | 1.95 |
| Participate actively in national higher education organizations | 3.45 | 3.77 |
| Dress well | 4.25 | 4.40 |
| Put my institution before myself | 4.26 | 4.15 |
| Appear confident even when in doubt | 3.98 | 4.13 |
| Am rarely seen as flamboyant | 3.68 | 3.49 |
| Believe fund-raising and development tasks are my highest priority | 3.24 | 3.44 |
| Am viewed by faculty as a strongly academic person | 3.67 | 3.80 |
| Have the strong support of my governing board | 4.67 | 4.44 |

(continued)

Table 5.2
(Continued)

| | | |
|---|---|---|
| Have successfully concluded many partnerships involving business and government with my institutions | 3.91 | 4.16 |
| Make many mistakes | 2.65 | 2.50 |
| Am solely responsible for teaching a course at least once every two years | 2.30 | 2.20 |
| Generate many innovative ideas | 4.17 | 4.35 |
| Believe faculty should make academic decisions | 3.93 | 4.04 |
| Am warm and affable | 4.02 | 4.18 |
| Believe intercollegiate athletics are in need of reform | 3.81 | 3.71 |
| Spend a great deal of time dealing with the media and the press | 2.93 | 3.05 |
| Am viewed by minorities and women as highly supportive of them | 4.21 | 4.42 |
| Am an internationalist in outlook | 3.95 | 4.11 |

seat-of-the-pants generalizations, for example, about the frequency of strong, even autocratic presidents of historically Black colleges and universities (HBCUs), the discussion sometimes is reminiscent of table gossip at the campus Starbucks.

We attempt to remedy some of those problems here. Table 5.2 presents data that summarize the major differences between the responses of minority presidents and those of Caucasian presidents. In order to make this task more manageable, only those differences that exhibit statistical significance at the .10 level or better are presented.

## MINORITY PRESIDENTS: A CLOSER LOOK AT PERSONAL CHARACTERISTICS

The most important thing to note is that there is less distance between minority presidents and nonminority, Caucasian presidents in terms of background and experience than exists between women and men presidents. By way of illustration, there are no statistically significant differences between minority and Caucasian presidents in terms of whether they hold the doctorate, how long they have been a president, how long they have served in their current presidency, or whether they have received an honorary degree. For example, 83.3 percent of Caucasian presidents hold an earned doctorate; 83.5 percent of minority presidents have the same status.

A few experience- and background-related differences do exist. For example, a slightly larger percent of Caucasian presidents advanced to their current position from another presidency, but this gap is not huge (77.4 percent versus 75.9 percent). And minority presidents are considerably more likely to have earned their baccalaureate degree from a public institution (59.5 percent versus 49.6 percent). If, as we argued earlier, prestigious independent liberal arts colleges frequently have served as the launching pad for college and university presidencies and often generate productive contacts that endure for a lifetime, then this differential is disadvantageous for minority presidents. Further, minority presidents have published fewer books and refereed journal articles than Caucasian presidents, though the gap is smaller than the one we observed between women and men presidents.

Let's summarize what we have just said. Relative to Caucasian presidents, minority presidents are *less likely* to

Have advanced to their current presidency from another presidency

Hold their baccalaureate degree from an independent institution

Have published as many books and refereed journal articles

On the other hand, minority presidents hold more memberships in national higher education organizations and are more likely to have held an office in one of those organizations. Also, they are even more likely than the presidents' group as a whole to be political Democrats (consistent with national data) and Roman Catholics. They are somewhat more likely than Caucasian presidents to be currently married and somewhat more likely to have a spouse who is employed full-time. Finally, they are more likely than Caucasian presidents to place heavy reliance on modern technology in their administrative tasks.

Let's summarize these relationships. Relative to Caucasian presidents, minority presidents are *more likely* to

Hold memberships in national higher education organizations

Have held office in such an organization

Identify themselves as political Democrats

Identify themselves as Roman Catholics

Be currently married

Have a spouse or significant other who works full-time

Place heavy reliance upon the use of modern technology administratively

In an overall sense, however, when compared to women presidents, minority presidents are more comparable in background to the Caucasian males who still dominate the ranks of college presidents. Differences exist in background and experience, but they are not huge. Plausibly, this accounts for the fact that minority presidents as a group are just about as likely as Caucasian presidents to have been nominated by an expert as an effective, outstanding president.

There are two instructive comparisons that will help solidify these points. The first comparison deals with objective characteristics often thought to describe essential presidential qualifications, while the second relates to marital characteristics that may be irrelevant, or even illegal to consider, in many situations (but which appear to make a difference).

Table 5.3 compares various groups of presidents in terms of the frequency with which they hold an earned doctorate, the number of years they have been presidents, and their published scholarship. Minority presidents exceed women presidents on all of these variables, and to the extent that the Ph.D. is a more desirable doctoral pedigree than an Ed.D., they surpass both men presidents and Caucasian presidents in this regard. Minority presidents have earned a doctorate almost as often as Caucasian presidents, and the length of their tenure in their current presidency is quite comparable. Thus, typical minority presidents do not operate at much of a disadvantage with respect to Caucasian presidents except in terms of their production of scholarly books and articles. And even here they are equal to, or better situated, than women presidents.

Table 5.3
Comparing Groups of Presidents in Terms of Experience and Background

| Characteristic | Caucasian Presidents | Men Presidents | Women Presidents | Minority Presidents |
|---|---|---|---|---|
| Hold an Earned Doctorate | 83.3% | 85.6% | 82.4% | 83.5% |
| Ph.D. | 56.9% | 59.6% | 50.7% | 66.6% |
| Ed.D. | 22.4% | 21.3% | 25.7% | 18.8% |
| Mean Years Spent In Current Presidency | 7.8 | 8.6 | 6.4 | 7.6 |
| Number of Books Published | 1.2 | 1.3 | 0.9 | 0.9 |
| Number of Refereed Journal Articles Published | 12.6 | 13.2 | 10.3 | 11.6 |

Table 5.4 examines the marital circumstances of these same groups of presidents. Many readers may argue that the marital circumstances of a president or a presidential candidate are irrelevant (and in all but a few cases illegal to take into consideration). We agree. Yet we note that the evidence we have presented suggests that many spouses can, and do, make a positive difference in the success of the president. Previously, we found that presidents whose spouses or significant others do not attend many campus events, or who work full-time, tend more often to be representative rather than effective presidents. As one can see in Table 5.4, these factors work to the disadvantage of women presidents in particular. The spouses or significant others of men presidents are more likely than those of women presidents to attend campus events; they are less likely to work full-time. Neither circumstance, our data tell us, is advantageous for women presidents.

We hasten to point out that marital status and spousal activities, by themselves, are not overwhelming determinants of presidential success. Many other things, including the president's values, interpersonal skills, energy, vision, and ability to generate innovative ideas are more pivotal in separating effective presidents from representative presidents. Nevertheless, women presidents who proclaim (perhaps somewhat tongue in cheek) in the fashion of one of our interviewees that, "Who needs a husband? He would simply get in my way" may be at odds with empirical evidence. In fact, a husband may not be particularly useful to a woman president; however, our evidence clearly suggests the opposite often is true, namely, wives often are helpful to men presidents. A sexist condition? Perhaps, but we would be less than honest if we did not point out these implications of our findings.

Spouses or significant others of minority presidents do not attend as many campus events. Also, a higher percentage of the spouses and signif-

Table 5.4
Comparing Groups of Presidents in Terms of Marital Circumstances

| Characteristic | Caucasian Presidents | Men Presidents | Women Presidents | Minority Presidents |
|---|---|---|---|---|
| Spouse or Significant Other Does Not Attend Many Events | 10.7% | 12.1% | 22.8% | 15.2% |
| Spouse or Significant Other is Employed Full-Time | 32.8% | 29.5% | 41.9% | 36.7% |

icant others of minority presidents are employed full-time than is true for Caucasian presidents. Minority presidents' spouses and significant others occupy the middle ground between men presidents and women presidents where these variables are concerned, but once again our data suggest these characteristics work to their disadvantage in terms of generating presidential effectiveness.

## MINORITY PRESIDENTS: A CLOSER LOOK AT INSTITUTIONAL CHARACTERISTICS

In contrast to personal characteristics, there are notable differences between the institutional characteristics of the colleges and universities of minority presidents and those of Caucasian presidents. When compared to the institutions in which Caucasian presidents operate, the institutions of minority presidents are *more likely* to

Be smaller in size (5,413 versus 6,041 student headcount)

Be publicly controlled

Have annual operating budgets that are only about one-half the size

Receive lower scores on the institutional peer rankings generated annually by *U.S. News and World Report*

Enroll students with lower mean ACT scores, lower rankings in their high school graduating classes, and lower high school grade point averages, though they do accept a lower percentage of their freshmen applicants

Retain a lower percentage of their students between their freshmen and sophomore years and graduate a lower percentage of their undergraduate students within six years of their matriculation

Offer a lower percentage of classes with fewer than 20 students

Have a lower percentage of full-time faculty

Raise less money in their annual funds, have a lower percentage of alumni who provide an annual gift, and have endowments that are less than one-fifth the size

In a nutshell, the colleges and universities in which minority presidents toil are smaller, less selective, and less well-heeled financially than those led by Caucasian presidents. This is hardly surprising in light of the fact that almost one-third of all minority college presidents lead a historically Black college or university (HBCU). HBCUs are notable for many outstanding achievements, including serving as a friendly and open portal for many students who later achieve at very high levels despite inadequate academic preparation. However, excepting a few institutions such as Hampton, Howard, and Spelman, HBCUs in general are not well endowed and frequently struggle financially. This is apparent in the institutional profile that we just have drawn.

## MINORITY PRESIDENTS: A CLOSER LOOK AT ATTITUDES, VALUES, AND BEHAVIOR

Relative to Caucasian presidents, minority presidents are *more likely* to

View themselves as hard-nosed

Believe in organizational structure

Believe in close collegial relationships with faculty

Believe in merit pay

Believe they are sometimes viewed as assertive

Use social and athletic functions as opportunities to promote their institutions

Believe they maintain a measure of mystique

Consider utilizing alternative methods of delivering higher education

Choose another CEO as a confidant

Participate actively in national higher education organizations

Dress well

Appear confident even when in doubt

Believe they are seen as flamboyant

Believe that fund-raising and development are their highest priorities

Believe that faculty view them as a strongly academic person

Have concluded many partnerships with business and government

Generate many innovative ideas

Believe faculty should make academic decisions

Believe they are seen as warm and affable

Spend a great deal of time dealing with the media and the press

Believe they are viewed as highly supportive of minorities and women

See themselves as internationalist in their outlook

Relative to Caucasian presidents, minority presidents are *less likely* to

Believe they frequently violate the status quo

Count committee meetings as a mistake

Believe they put their institutions before themselves

Believe they have the strong support of their governing boards

Believe they make many mistakes

Be solely responsible for teaching a course at least once every two years

Believe intercollegiate athletics are in need of reform

## MINORITY PRESIDENTS: DRAWING CONCLUSIONS

While minority college presidents are by and large similar to Caucasian presidents in terms of demographic characteristics such as age, degree status, and experience, they differ considerably in terms of the characteristics of the institutions they lead, as well as in certain of their attitudes, values, and behavior. It is apparent that minority presidents are a complex group, perhaps because they are so diverse. They tell us they are often hard-nosed, assertive, somewhat bureaucratic individuals who are confident, even flamboyant, and believe they seldom make mistakes. Frequently, they are driven individuals who describe themselves as less likely than Caucasian presidents to put their institutions before their own welfare. This fits with the strong, autocratic, even fatherly image that frequently is evoked to describe HBCU presidents (Gaona, 2003). It is less clear that this generalization fits Asian American and Hispanic American presidents. Our relatively small samples (only three Asian American presidents and 33 Hispanic American presidents) do not permit strong inferences in this arena. Yet it is plausible that African American presidents may differ from other minority presidents on these variables.

On the other hand, relative to Caucasian presidents, minority presidents more often believe they are seen as warm and affable and are more likely to believe committee meetings are useful. They often pursue highly external presidencies and spend larger amounts of time with the media and the press than do Caucasian presidents. They confess that they attempt to use nearly every social or athletic occasion to promote their institutions. They are accomplished networkers who utilize professional meetings as opportunities to meet and greet others, learn, and further their agendas.

Relative to Caucasian presidents, minority presidents are less likely to believe that intercollegiate athletics is in need of reform. This may reflect the considerable emphasis that many HBCUs place on intercollegiate athletics, sometimes to the dismay of outsiders.

It is intriguing that minority presidents, compared to Caucasian presidents, are less confident that they have the strong support of their governing boards. This may or may not be attributable to their ethnic status. It is possible that minority presidents feel less comfortable with governing boards that are dominated by nonminority members. However, our own inspection of our data did not reveal a difference between the presidents of HBCUs (which are more likely to have minority-dominated governing boards) and other majority institutions on this score.

We noted earlier that a disproportionate number of African American presidents were nominated by our experts as being especially successful and effective. On the other hand, other ethnic groups (Asian Americans and Hispanic Americans) were underrepresented in the effective president category. We have no ready explanation for this, and our sample sizes are not sufficient for us to apply our usual statistical tests with confidence.

## SUMMING UP OUR EVIDENCE CONCERNING WOMEN AND MINORITY PRESIDENTS

Women and men presidents differ in a variety of ways. Most obviously, the demographic profiles of women and men presidents, while converging in recent years, still differ visibly in critical areas relating to education, experience, and scholarship. We hypothesize that these differences will disappear as time passes. On the other hand, the demographic dichotomy between minority presidents and Caucasian presidents is not as great, and minority presidents and Caucasian presidents have similar portfolios with respect to their degree status and their experience as presidents.

Do the attitudes, values, and activities of women and minority presidents differ from those of similarly situated nonminority men presidents? Yes and no, and when differences do exist, they are not always in the direction predicted by those who believe that women presidents and perhaps minority presidents are more likely to evince a "caring, sharing" model of administration. Women presidents appear to be more committed to consensus-seeking behavior than men and more likely to believe in the efficacy of their faculty senates. They are less likely to believe in merit pay. They are less likely to believe they constitute the final authority on the campus under their governing board. However, perhaps surprising to some, they value one-on-one meetings less than men presidents and are less likely to delegate responsibilities. They are more supportive than men presidents of the notion that effective leaders take risks. A higher proportion of women than men presidents regard themselves as warm and affable individuals who smile a lot. They tend to use modern administrative technologies more than men.

Minority presidents may adhere more often to what Chliwniak (1997) and others perceive to be the stereotypical male model of management. In their own estimation, minority presidents are hard-nosed, confident, often assertive leaders who do not believe they make many mistakes. As is the case for women presidents, they believe they are warm and affable individuals who occasionally are flamboyant (at least compared to the usual male president). Both women and minority presidents are more likely than men presidents and Caucasian presidents to seek advice from another CEO in order to improve their job performance and to network at off-campus higher education meetings. They may feel more in need of mentors, counsel, and support than the stereotypical Caucasian male president.

Yet, on the majority of the more than 60 items with which we probed presidential attitudes, values, and behavior, we did not find statistically significant differences between women and men presidents, or between minority and Caucasian presidents. Most presidents tend to see issues and values in much the same light, or there is no consistent pattern of difference. And, with a few exceptions, they tend to behave in substantially similar ways. *Hence, our overall evidence is only modestly supportive of the notion that women and minority presidents actually behave differently from men presidents.* Just as demographic convergence has been occurring between women and men presidents relative to experience and other variables, it may well be that values and behavioral convergence between women and men presidents, and minority and Caucasian presidents, is occurring as well. Why so? It may be that as the American college presidency has become more accessible to women and minorities, and the interchange between various groups of presidents has increased, that this has provided all presidents with greater opportunities to observe each other and in a pragmatic sense to see what works. Astute presidents then draw both theoretical and practical conclusions from their observations, borrow notions they find attractive, and gradually modify their views and actions. It is learning by doing in a classic sense, and it extends to men and Caucasian presidents[5] as well as to women and minority presidents.

That said, perhaps the most important area where significant differences exist between groups of presidents is in the area of entrepreneurial attitudes, values, and behavior. These differences are sufficiently important to the determination of presidential success that we will devote all of chapter 6 to exploring them.

# CHAPTER 6

# The Entrepreneurial President: Statistical Tests

What would life be if we had no courage to attempt anything?
—Vincent Van Gogh, nineteenth-century Dutch painter

A person who walks in another's tracks leaves no footprints.
—Anonymous

Example is always more efficacious than precept.
—Samuel Johnson, eighteenth-century English author

The statistical tests reported in chapters 4 and 5 have set the stage for our examination of specific hypotheses that focus upon the entrepreneurial characteristics of college presidents. We have selected 11 specific hypotheses that relate to entrepreneurial attitudes, values, and behavior. The question we seek to answer is straightforward—Do effective presidents differ from representative presidents with respect to entrepreneurism and, if so, how?

## THE ENTREPRENEURIAL HYPOTHESES

In order to test the notion that some presidents are more entrepreneurial than others, we developed a set of 11 hypotheses that bear upon entrepreneurial attitudes, values, and behavior. These are listed in Table 6.1. We label seven of these hypotheses *hard* in the sense that they relate primarily to entrepreneurial actions identified by Peck (1983) and Hesselbein and Johnston

Table 6.1
The Entrepreneurial Hypotheses

| The Hypotheses | One-Tailed Probability of a Statistically Significant Difference Between the Responses of Effective Presidents and Representative Presidents |
|---|---|
| • **The "Hard" Entrepreneurial Hypotheses** | |
| 1) Believe that an effective leader takes risks | .143 |
| 2) Have made decisions that could have resulted in my losing my job if the result had turned out badly | .081 |
| 3) Frequently violate the *status quo* | .009 |
| 4) Enjoy stirring things up | .342 |
| 5) Generate many innovative ideas | .000 |
| 6) Have successfully concluded many partnerships involving business and government with my institutions | .000 |
| 7) Am more likely than most presidents to consider alternative methods of delivering higher education | .016 |
| • **The "Soft" Entrepreneurial Hypotheses** | |
| 8) Believe in organizational structure | .000 |
| 9) Often like people who are different | .054 |
| 10) Encourage creative individuals even though we may disagree | .293 |
| 11) Am internationalist in outlook | .000 |

*Note:* The table assumes that effective presidents are more entrepreneurial than representative presidents. Thus, for example, we assume that effective presidents generate more innovative ideas, and we find this to be true. In this case, the difference between the responses of effective presidents and representative presidents are statistically significant at the .000 level. In fact, in every instance, effective presidents respond more entrepreneurially than representative presidents. That is, the expected sign of the difference between the two groups is always consistent with our a priori prediction. Because we do have an a priori prediction, we utilize a one-tailed test of statistical significance. Not all of the differences are statistically significant. However, five of the seven hard hypotheses are statistically significant at the .10 level or better, and three of the four soft hypotheses meet the same standard.

(2002a). The remaining four hypotheses we deem *soft* in that they represent presidential attitudes and receptive environments that entrepreneurial presidents might encourage or create. If the campus environment is open and receptive to new approaches, and not only tolerates but also encourages unusual individuals or unconventional approaches, then arguably more entrepreneurial activity will take place. The president must foster a friendly, cultivating environment for entrepreneurial activity. Hence, her attitudes and values in this arena transmit loud and important signals to all concerned about the receptivity of the president and the campus to change.

The notable message of Table 6.1 is the strong support it provides the entrepreneurial hypotheses. The signs on all 11 relationships are as predicted by those who argue that effective presidents are entrepreneurial in outlook and behavior. That is, the difference between the means of the variables for effective and representative presidents is always in the direction that entrepreneurial theory forecasts. For example, consider hypothesis 6: "I have successfully concluded many partnerships involving business and government with my institutions." In Table 4.1, we saw that the mean response of effective presidents was 4.15, while the mean response of representative presidents was only 3.72. This difference is statistically significant at the .000 level and presents persuasive evidence that effective presidents behave differently—more entrepreneurially—than representative presidents.

In each of the 11 cases, then, the expected responses of effective presidents differ from those of representative presidents in the direction entrepreneurial advocates predict. Four of the 11 relationships are statistically significant at the .000 level. Six of the 11 relationships are statistically significant at the .10 level or better, and 8 of 11 are statistically significant at the .162 level or better.

These results support two conclusions:

The data provide considerable support for the notion that a distinctive class of entrepreneurial presidents exists.

The data demonstrate that effective presidents tend to be entrepreneurial in character. Indeed, it is difficult for presidents to be perceived as successful if they do not possess entrepreneurial attitudes and values and behave entrepreneurially.

Upon reflection, perhaps it should not be surprising that effective presidents believe in taking risks, generate many innovative ideas, are skillful in concluding partnerships with nonacademic bodies, violate the status quo, do not allow organizational structure to stifle their institutions, often like people who are different, or tend to be internationalists in their personal outlook. These are all characteristics that one would associate instinctively with activist, visionary (yes, entrepreneurial) leaders who transform their organizations.

## GROUP COMPARISONS OF ENTREPRENEURIAL CHARACTERISTICS

Are entrepreneurial characteristics uniformly distributed across presidents? That is, do all of the major subgroups of presidents we have examined have much the same entrepreneurial instincts and behave in an equally entrepreneurial fashion? Our data suggest the answer to these questions is no. As Tables 6.2 and 6.3 demonstrate, there are substantial differences between presidential cohorts in terms of their entrepreneurial attitudes, values, and behavior. Consider Table 6.2, where the mean responses of six subgroups of college presidents are compared to the group as a whole. Consider hypothesis 3, "I frequently violate the status quo," as an illustration. The mean response of all presidents is 3.84, while it is 3.92 for effective presidents, but only 3.75 for representative presidents. Women presidents register a 3.91 score, while minority presidents record only a 3.72 score. Thus, according to this criterion, effective presidents and women presidents are more entrepreneurial in character than representa-

Table 6.2
The Entrepreneurial Hypotheses: Group Comparisons

| The Hypotheses | | All | Eff | Rep | Men | Wom | Cauc | Min |
|---|---|---|---|---|---|---|---|---|
| • The "Hard" Entrepreneurial Hypotheses | | | | | | | | |
| 1) | Believe that an effective leader takes risks | 4.70 | 4.73 | 4.66 | 4.68 | 4.79 | 4.70 | 4.72 |
| 2) | Have made decisions that could have resulted in my losing my job if the result had turned out badly | 3.99 | 4.01 | 3.96 | 4.01 | 4.04 | 3.99 | 3.92 |
| 3) | Frequently violate the *status quo* | 3.84 | 3.92 | 3.75 | 3.82 | 3.91 | 3.84 | 3.72 |
| 4) | Enjoy stirring things up | 3.12 | 3.14 | 3.11 | 3.14 | 3.05 | 3.11 | 3.06 |
| 5) | Generate many innovative ideas | 4.19 | 4.28 | 4.08 | 4.19 | 4.17 | 4.17 | 4.15 |
| 6) | Have successfully concluded many partnerships involving business and government with my institutions | 3.94 | 4.15 | 3.72 | 3.95 | 3.91 | 3.91 | 4.01 |
| 7) | Am more likely than most presidents to consider alternative methods of delivering higher education | 3.58 | 3.64 | 3.51 | 3.58 | 3.57 | 3.55 | 3.67 |
| • The "Soft" Entrepreneurial Hypotheses | | All | Eff | Rep | Men | Wom | Cauc | Min |
| 8) | Believe in organizational structure | 4.09 | 3.98 | 4.21 | 4.10 | 4.05 | 4.12 | 4.28 |
| 9) | Often like people who are different | 4.03 | 4.07 | 3.98 | 3.99 | 4.18 | 4.01 | 3.96 |
| 10) | Encourage creative individuals even though we may disagree | 4.42 | 4.43 | 4.39 | 4.41 | 4.46 | 4.41 | 4.42 |
| 11) | Am internationalist in outlook | 3.98 | 4.10 | 3.86 | 3.39 | 3.97 | 3.95 | 4.11 |

tive presidents and minority presidents, with men and Caucasian presidents[1] falling in the middle.

An inspection of the data in Table 6.2 reveals that effective presidents and women presidents tend to exhibit the more pronounced entrepreneurial scores, while representative presidents and minority presidents occupy the other end of the scale. Table 6.3 provides rankings that summarize these relationships. When we include all presidents, we have seven different groups of presidents; Table 6.3 ranks the mean responses of each of these groups, first through seventh, on the entrepreneurial scale.

Focusing only on the hard entrepreneurial hypotheses for a moment, we can see from Table 6.3 that effective presidents rank fourth in terms of hypothesis 1, which focuses on risk taking, second in terms of hypothesis 2, which focuses on decision making that might have cost the president his job, and so forth. The sum of the ranks for effective presidents here is 12; compare this to 25 for all presidents and 40 for representative presidents. The lower the sum, the more entrepreneurial a group of presidents. Accordingly, we see that the sum of the ranks is 19 for men presidents, 25 for women presidents, 32 for Caucasian presidents, and 35 for minority presidents. Thus, within this group of hard hypotheses, which tend to focus on actual behavior, effective presidents are the most entrepreneurial and minority and representative presidents the least entrepreneurial.

Moving next to the soft hypotheses, we see once again that the effective presidents exhibit the lowest rank sum (7) and representative presidents the highest (25). This set of hypotheses focuses primarily on attitudinal characteristics.

We can compute an overall sum of the ranks by putting the two sets of hypotheses together. The lowest rank sum (19) is recorded by effective presidents, making them the most entrepreneurial of all of the groups. The highest sum (52) is recorded by representative presidents, making them the least entrepreneurial of all of the groups. If one subscribes to the view that entrepreneurial attitudes, values and behavior are essential to presidential success, then these results make it crystal clear why some presidents are perceived to be very successful and others less so. *Clearly, effective presidents are entrepreneurial in character, and we believe this is a most important reason why experts consider them to be successful and effective. Similarly, it is not easy to avoid concluding that representative presidents (those who have not been designated by an expert as especially successful or effective) have been relegated to that category because they are not sufficiently entrepreneurial in outlook and behavior.*

*Thus, our results provide significant support for the notion of the entrepreneurial leader. These results give empirical substance to the usually anecdotal*

Table 6.3
The Entrepreneurial Hypotheses: Ranking Group Responses

### The Hypotheses

| | The "Hard" Entrepreneurial Hypotheses | All | Eff | Rep | Men | Wom | Cauc | Min |
|---|---|---|---|---|---|---|---|---|
| 1) | Believe that an effective leader takes risks | 6 | 4 | 3 | 2 | 1 | 6 | 5 |
| 2) | Have made decisions that could have resulted in my losing my job if the result had turned out badly | 4 | 2 | 6 | 2 | 1 | 4 | 7 |
| 3) | Frequently violate the *status quo* | 3 | 1 | 6 | 5 | 2 | 3 | 7 |
| 4) | Enjoy stirring things up | 3 | 1 | 4 | 1 | 7 | 4 | 6 |
| 5) | Generate many innovative ideas | 2 | 1 | 7 | 3 | 4 | 4 | 6 |
| 6) | Have successfully concluded many partnerships involving business and government with my institutions | 4 | 1 | 7 | 3 | 6 | 4 | 2 |
| 7) | Am more likely than most presidents to consider alternative methods of delivering higher education | 3 | 2 | 7 | 3 | 5 | 5 | 1 |
| | **Sum of the Ranks "Hard" Hypotheses** | **25** | **12** | **40** | **19** | **26** | **30** | **34** |
| | **The "Soft" Entrepreneurial Hypotheses** | **All** | **Eff** | **Rep** | **Men** | **Wom** | **Cauc** | **Min** |
| 8) | Believe in organizational structure | 3 | 1 | 6 | 4 | 2 | 5 | 7 |
| 9) | Often like people who are different | 3 | 2 | 6 | 5 | 1 | 4 | 7 |
| 10) | Encourage creative individuals even though we may disagree | 3 | 2 | 7 | 5 | 1 | 5 | 3 |
| 11) | Am internationalist in outlook | 3 | 2 | 6 | 7 | 4 | 4 | 1 |
| | **Sum of the Ranks "Soft Hypotheses"** | **12** | **7** | **25** | **21** | **8** | **18** | **18** |
| | **Sum of the Ranks "Soft" and "Hard" Hypotheses** | **37** | **19** | **65** | **40** | **34** | **48** | **52** |
| | **Overall Ranking** | **3rd** | **1st** | **7th** | **4th** | **2nd** | **5th** | **6th** |

*Note:* The table ranks each group's response. In 10 of the 11 cases, the highest score receives the highest ranking (first) and the lowest score receives the lowest ranking (seventh). The exception is "Believe in organizational structure." The more a president believes in organizational structure, the less entrepreneurial she is likely to be. Hence, in this case, the lowest score receives the highest ranking (first) and the highest score receives the lowest ranking (seventh).

*and often normative speculations of hundreds of writers in the past about the nature of leadership and its connection to entrepreneurial attitudes, values, and behavior. Yes, a distinctive class of entrepreneurial leaders does exist. Further, these entrepreneurial leaders, who are innovative, flexible risk takers who are not afraid to violate the status quo, are more successful than nonentrepreneurial leaders, at least as experts see their performance. And, finally, these generalizations visibly apply to college presidents. Successful presidents tend to be entrepreneurial and vice versa.*

Contained within our explorations concerning entrepreneurial leadership, which are summarized in Table 6.3, are some fascinating and thought-provoking results. *All things considered, women presidents are more entrepreneurial than men presidents, especially in their attitudes and values.* For example, women presidents rank substantially higher than men presidents with respect to how they perceive their own willingness to encourage creative individuals with whom they may disagree.

The woman president of a large public university whom we interviewed suggested that women presidents must be more flexible and entrepreneurial in order to deal with the vicissitudes of academic life and leadership. They cannot count upon some of the long-established connections that men presidents may have, she argued, and must find different ways to skin the cat.

Our data also speak to the relative absence of entrepreneurial character among minority presidents. *Ceteris paribus, minority presidents are less likely than men, women, and Caucasian presidents to exhibit entrepreneurial attitudes, values, and behavior, and they fall substantially short of effective presidents in this regard.* Consider hypothesis 3, "I frequently violate the status quo." Minority presidents rank seventh (last) on this criterion, while effective presidents rank first, women presidents second, and Caucasian presidents third. The pointed comment made to us by the African American president of a majority institution perhaps encapsulates the feelings of many minority presidents: "If I veer too far out of the box and make too many mistakes, I'll get canned. It's that simple."

Many minority presidents may be risk averse. In previous work, we speculated that minority presidents "may have a tendency to avoid major risk-taking activities" (Fisher and Koch, 1996, 92), and we now have found evidence to support this conjecture. As Stephen Carter argued in his *Reflections of an Affirmative Action Baby* (1992), minority leaders are always vexingly in the spotlight. It is difficult for some to avoid mumbled commentary in the background that, absent their race, they might not have been appointed. Thus, they feel they must perform at an above-average level to avoid the subtle, but damaging stigma that may be attached to so-called affirmative action appointees. This may lead to a culture emphasizing risk-averse behavior. Don't put your job in jeopardy by climbing out on a limb; don't take unnecessary chances.

Of course, most readers will join the authors in generating counterexamples to these broad generalizations. An African American president told us he did not believe the results would apply to the same extent to HBCUs. At most HBCUs, he pointed out, minority faculty, staff, and administrators are in fact the majority ethnic group, and generally this ethnic mix extends to membership on the HBCU governing boards. While broader public and societal scrutiny still applies to HBCUs, in theory there is a greater opportunity for an HBCU president to carve her own path and to worry less about what the Caucasian establishment and power elite may think. Even so, we did not find significant differences between HBCU presidents and other minority presidents in terms of their entrepreneurial behavior.

With our having registered those caveats, it nonetheless remains true that the typical minority college president is not as entrepreneurial as most other groups of presidents. Although minority presidents clearly are different from our representative, less successful presidents in many ways, they are closer to them demographically than any other group of presidents we have examined. The growing confidence of minority presidents in their own performance and their greater acceptance by the larger society may in the future fuel greater entrepreneurial behavior on their part. Given our data and analysis, we believe it is critical that this transformation occur, for the lesser commitment of minority presidents to entrepreneurial attitudes, values, and behavior works to their disadvantage. By contrast, women presidents are vigorously entrepreneurial in many ways, and our analysis suggests this is clearly related to their success.

## MULTIVARIATE ANALYSIS OF ENTREPRENEURIAL RELATIONSHIPS

We cautioned in an earlier chapter that bivariate relationships sometimes are altered or even disappear when multivariate analysis is conducted. For example, we hypothesized that the disproportionately low appearance of women presidents in the effective president category was due to their demographic characteristics and resulting visibility (items which will change over time) rather than to some innate lack of suitability or competence. We will now demonstrate this is in fact the case and in so doing will shed additional light on our entrepreneurial hypotheses.

Table 6.4 reports the results of a multivariate logistic regression in which the dependent variable we wish to explain is a 0,1 categorical dummy variable indicating whether or not a president falls into either the effective or

Table 6.4
Multivariate Analysis of Presidential Success: Logistic Regression Model

| Independent Variable | Regression Coefficient | Wald Statistic | Statistical Significance* | Beta Coefficient |
|---|---|---|---|---|
| Institutional Control Variables | | | | |
| Hdcount enrolment | .000 | 8.99 | .002 | 1.00 |
| Institutional control (1 if public) | -.610 | 1.45 | .115 | .54 |
| SAT verbal midrange | .010 | 8.44 | .002 | 1.01 |
| Personal Control Variables | | | | |
| N Membersh Nat'l. | .603 | 13.86 | .000 | 1.83 |
| Teach course | -.142 | 1.17 | .140 | .87 |
| Yrs higher educ | -.015 | .38 | .267 | .99 |
| Yrs current presidency | .081 | 7.29 | .004 | 1.09 |
| Gender (1 = woman) | -.185 | .15 | .350 | .83 |
| Race (1 = Caucasian) | .025 | .00 | .480 | 1.03 |
| Computer use (1 = heavy) | -.323 | .26 | .306 | .72 |
| Values, Attitudes and Behavior | | | | |
| High value consensus | .810 | 9.67 | .001 | 2.25 |
| Close collegial rel | .028 | .02 | .443 | 1.03 |
| Board micromanages | -.024 | .02 | .447 | .98 |
| Entrepreneurial Hypotheses | | | | |
| Eff leaders take risks | .591 | 2.44 | .059 | 1.81 |
| Believe org structure | -1.33 | 16.79 | .000 | .265 |
| Violate status quo | .320 | 2.84 | .046 | 1.38 |
| Many partnerships with business and govt. | .177 | 1.06 | .152 | 1.19 |

The dependent variable is a 0,1 categorical dummy variable in which a 0 is assigned to every president who was not nominated as especially effective (representative) and a 1 is assigned to every president who was nominated (effective).

*One-tailed test of statistical significance because each independent variable has a predicted sign.

Constant: −9.72 (Wald = 9.12, statistical significance = .002)

−2 Log Likelihood: 222.3

Nagelkerke $R^2$: .425

Equation chi-square: 88.47 (Significance = .000)

N: 240

the representative category. For every president in our sample, then, the value of the dependent variable is 1 if the president has been nominated as successful and effective and 0 otherwise (signifying a representative president).

We seek to explain the differences between effective and representative presidents on the basis of several categories of variables:

## Institutional Control Variables

Our intent here is to include explanatory variables that take into account institutional characteristics that might influence presidential reputation. Based upon our bivariate analyses in chapters 4 and 5, there are three institutional characteristics that seem most relevant:

1. *Headcount Enrollment:* Size may confer visibility, reputation, and valuable social distance; we predict a positive sign on the regression coefficient of this variable.
2. *Institutional Control:* This variable, which assumes a value of 1 if the institution is public, addresses the nature of institutional control. We predict a negative sign, believing that independent status confers a reputational advantage, *ceteris paribus*.
3. *SAT Verbal Midrange Score for Entering Freshmen:* The quality of the institution's student body may positively influence perceptions of the president, and hence we predict a positive sign.

## Personal Control Variables

Our intent here is to include key explanatory variables that relate to the president's personal background, experience, and behavior.

*Number of Active Memberships in National Higher Education Organizations:* More memberships yield greater visibility, and therefore we predict a positive sign.

*Solely Responsible for Teaching a Course at Least Once Every Two Years:* Teaching, especially if the president is solely responsible for teaching a course, is a tremendous demand on a president's time and, however praiseworthy, may detract from other duties. We predict a negative sign.

*Total Number of Years Spent in Higher Education:* This variable measures higher education experience, but in addition it implicitly measures the extent of presidential visibility and contacts. We predict a positive sign.

*Years in Current Presidency:* The larger the number of years a president has spent in her presidency, the more experience she has, and hence we predict a positive sign.

*Gender:* This variable assumes a value of 1 if the president is a woman. Once demographic variables have been considered, we do not believe gender is an important predictor of reputation and performance. Therefore, we do not expect the coefficient of this variable to achieve statistical significance.

*Race/Ethnic Background:* This variable assumes a value of 1 if the president is Caucasian. Once demographic variables have been taken into account, we do not expect ethnic status to be an important predictor of reputation and performance. Thus, we do not expect the coefficient of this variable to achieve statistical significance.

*Computer Use:* This variable measures whether the president says he uses a computer frequently. It is a proxy for all of the technology variables we introduced in chapter 4. We expect a negative sign, based upon the notion that excessive use of technology detracts from other presidential responsibilities, especially those of an interpersonal nature.

## Attitudes, Values, and Behavior

Our intent here is to include explanatory variables that describe key presidential attitudes and values.

*Place a High Value on Consensus:* While excessive attempts to achieve consensus could lead to dithering and a lack of action, holding other things constant, the attainment of consensus is quite helpful to a president, and therefore we expect a positive sign.

*Believe in Close Collegial Relationships with Faculty:* This is an FTW variable. FTW argued that when presidents maintain close collegial relationships with faculty, this gradually reduces the social distance between them and faculty and subtly erodes their authority. Based upon FTW, we expect a negative sign.

*Governing Board Micromanages:* FTW and other observers of the presidential scene believe that governing boards that mix policy-making and administration, and persistently interfere with the president's management of the institution, reduce the effectiveness of the president. Thus, we predict a negative sign.

## Entrepreneurial Hypotheses

Our intent here is to include explanatory variables that test the major aspects of the entrepreneurial hypotheses.

*Believe that an Effective Leader Takes Risks:* Intelligent risk taking is fundamental to entrepreneurial behavior. Earlier in this chapter, we established a strong connection between entrepreneurial behavior and presidential effectiveness. Hence, we predict a positive sign.

*Believe in Organizational Structure:* Following Peck (1983) and others, we allow for the possibility that rigid organizational structure can be a major impediment to change. Institutional transformation often requires presidents to develop ad hoc approaches to problems and issues and to find ways to tweak or circumvent their own organizations. Therefore, we predict a negative sign; the greater the belief in organizational structure, the less likely the president is to be entrepreneurial and successful.

*Frequently Violate the Status Quo:* Entrepreneurial, successful presidents must be willing to do things differently and to violate the status quo. Therefore, we predict a positive sign.

*Have Successfully Concluded Many Partnerships Involving Business and Government with My Institution:* Entrepreneurial activity by a president virtually requires that he find productive ways to cooperate and leverage resources with other institutions. Those that are unsuccessful on this count are also likely to be unsuccessful as presidents. We predict a positive sign.

The empirical results reported in Table 6.4 are strong and on the whole confirm our previous analysis and speculations. In the realm of institutional influences on presidential effectiveness, the larger the institution and the higher the quality of its student body (as measured by SAT scores), the more likely a president is to be considered effective. Both of the coefficients on these variables are statistically significant at the .002 level. The strong results with respect to institutional size are supportive of two hypotheses: (1) size confers visibility and increases the probability that one's presidential achievements will become known, and (2) size provides social distance and therefore enhances a president's ability to be successful.

The institutional control variable almost attains statistical significance at the .10 level. The sign on the coefficient of this variable is negative, indicating that independent institutional control, holding other things constant, is an advantage in terms of external perceptions of performance. The performance of the institutional control variables underlines the reality that perceptions of presidential performance cannot be easily separated from the reputations of their institutions. Larger, more prestigious institutions generate more publicity, and this influences presidential reputations. And independent status confers some prestige, independent of all other factors. The bottom line is that those who evaluate institutions and presidents implicitly seem to confer on an institution's president the perceived characteristics of that president's institution. If it is good, then she is often assumed to be good. The search-and-screen process for presidents "winnows down the field to the really capable," suggested a search firm executive we talked with who argued that the presidents of large and prestigious institutions are among the most capable individuals in higher education. This may often be the case; however, our findings also suggest that there is a halo cast by an institution above its president, who may or may not be a ball of fire.

The influence of visibility is also present in the Personal Control Variables category. The more national higher education organizations an individual president actively patronizes, the more visible he is and the more he is considered to be effective. Of course, it is possible that such activities actually provide presidents with knowledge and information that genuinely is of value and makes them more productive. However, the typical national higher education meeting may be more useful as a networking opportunity for presidents, while simultaneously serving as an expense-paid junket to a warm climate during the cold season. Whichever is the case, active participation in national higher education organizations is a distinct positive for being noted as an effective president.

Those presidents who assume sole responsibility for teaching a course at least once every two years are less likely to be included in the effective president category. The coefficient of this variable is negative, though it is statistically significant only at the .140 level. Some faculty may find this result hard to accept, for they consistently argue that presidents must not lose their connection to the faculty or lose sight of the fundamental academic nature of colleges and universities. Notwithstanding this view, we believe our finding underlines the changing nature of the American college presidency, which increasingly is externally oriented and ever more frequently requires the president to undertake significant fund-raising, public relations, and political tasks. One of the authors taught at least one course per year during every year of his two presidencies. He enjoyed doing so and was praised by faculty for his efforts. Still, it is not abundantly clear that this teaching was a good institutional investment of his time, although it may have conferred therapeutic benefits on him as a means to escape the incessant humdrum of presidential affairs. Our results suggest that presidents and governing boards should cast a jaundiced eye upon high levels of presidential teaching and research activity if their highest priority is presidential and institutional performance.[2]

Two of our personal control variables measure presidential experience. The coefficients of both variables have the positive signs we expected—increased experience makes it more likely that a president will be considered effective. The years in current presidency variable is statistically significant at the .004 level. The bottom line is, experience counts in the

American college presidency. While the relationship between experience and performance is not foolproof, individuals are usually more effective in their second presidency than in their first presidency. Of course, some presidents never become effective, experienced or not.

How does experience count? We believe presidential behavior is characterized by what economists call an error-learning model. Wise presidents consult, take actions, observe the results, and then modify their results accordingly, almost as an automobile driver does as she motors down the street. Modifications in presidential behavior frequently reflect a degree of experimentation and the process of finding a presidential comfort zone, that is, discovering those activities and approaches that best fit the president and her institution. Of course, all institutions are not the same, and even though there are some principles and actions that seem almost universal, what works on one campus may not work on another. Nonetheless, both overall higher education experience and campus-specific experience are usually valuable and increase presidential productivity.[3]

Gender and race are nonfactors as determinants of presidential effectiveness. The coefficient on the gender variable is negative (indicating femaleness is a disadvantage), but the relationship is not statistically significant. The one-tailed level of statistical significance is .350, and statistical significance falls to .700 for a two-tailed test, which is appropriate if one takes an agnostic view about the expected relationship. These are not eye-opening results. This finding supports our previous hypothesis that it is not femaleness per se that causes women to be included less often as effective presidents, but their distinctive demographics and individual behaviors. From chapter 4, we are aware that the degree status of women presidents differs from that of men, as does their experience level. Further, institutions led by women typically are smaller, less prestigious, and more likely to be limited to two years. These factors, which we believe will change as time passes, are the primary reasons why women do not fare as well as men when effective presidents are nominated. Discrimination may indeed be present, for example, in presidential appointments, and it may influence the demographics women bring to their presidency (for example, what universities they attended or disciplines they studied). However, once a woman has been appointed as a president, discrimination does not appear to be substantial in determining whether she is considered successful and effective.

The coefficient on the race variable fails to achieve statistical significance (.480 for a one-tailed test and .960 for a two-tailed test). As might be the case for women, race may have something to do with whether a minority individual is appointed to a presidency in the first place. Once appointed, however, there is no evidence that a president's ethnic background influences the extent to which that president is considered successful and effective.

As detailed earlier, it is not clear that strong use of technology by a president is advantageous. The negative coefficient on the computer use variable supports this caveat. Note, however, that the coefficient of the computer use variable is statistically significant only at the .306 level. Thus, we should not attempt to make too much of this finding. Nevertheless, the consistency of our finding should constitute a red flag to presidents and governing boards. Excessive reliance upon technology and/or excessive presidential time spent in front of a computer screen may be deleterious to performance.

The Values, Attitudes, and Behavior variables attempt to test hypotheses about presidential performance and effectiveness that have been offered by other authors and experts. Consensus seeking, as an illustration, is an oft-praised presidential activity, and our analysis suggests that those presidents who place strong emphasis upon achieving consensus are much more likely to be considered effective. This relationship is statistically significant at the .001 level, and the beta coefficient on this variable (indicating the relative importance of this relationship as opposed to the statistical significance of the estimate) is the highest of any independent variable.

Hence, it is apparent that consensus seeking is a valuable activity for presidents, and many presidents, especially those who tend toward authoritarian approaches, would increase their effectiveness were they to devote more attention to achieving campus consensus. What does not follow, of course, is that limiting one's actions to those that eventually achieve consensus campus support is similarly productive. In times of institutional crisis, consensus may be impossible to achieve, and presidents who move only after consensus has been achieved tend to produce institutional paralysis. Winston Churchill's famous derogatory comment about the problem of respecting politicians who keep their ears pinned to the ground (see the first page of chapter 2) comes to mind. Those leaders who slavishly follow the consensus of the crowd ultimately are apt to be regarded as good fellows but ineffectual leaders. There is, then, a golden mean to be pursued where presidential searches for consensus are concerned.

The variable representing presidential tendencies to maintain collegial relationships with faculty has a positive sign (the opposite of the FTW prediction), but it is statistically significant only at the .443 level. This variable may represent one aspect of social distance. The discussion over psychological distance and power relationships has been controversial. Fisher (1984) argues that intimacy erodes leadership because it tends to focus a harsh light on presidential weaknesses and obliterate charisma. As the mentor of one of the authors once pithily observed, "You can't drink beer every night with people and then expect them to regard you as their leader."

Whether or not the reader agrees with the distance argument, we find mixed evidence of it here. The institutional size variable, which is a plausible measure of presidential social distance, performs quite well. The collegial relationships variable does not. Hence, we must reserve our judgment. It is admittedly difficult to explain the concept of presidential distance, much less measure it. We do note, however, that minority presidents in particular are of the opinion that they have developed a certain level of mystique on their campuses (see chapter 5).

The final variable in this category asks presidents whether they believe their board is guilty of micromanagement. Those presidents who averred that this is true are less likely to appear on the effective president list (the coefficient is negative), but the relationship is statistically significant only at the .447 level. Micromanagement is a concept that is difficult to define, but it would seem to relate to situations where governing boards stray from making policy and become involved in the day-to-day administration of their institutions. Potentially, this destroys presidential credibility. In any case, we do not find evidence of that phenomenon here, though our method of measurement is rather crude.

We entered variables representing four different aspects of the entrepreneurial hypotheses in our predictive equation. Each of the coefficients of these variables assumes the sign that we predicted a priori, and each is statistically significant at the .152 level or better. Once again, but now more impressively in a multivariate context in which numerous other possible factors are being held constant, we find that

Effective leaders take risks.

Effective leaders do not believe heavily in organizational structure.

Effective leaders frequently violate the status quo.

Effective leaders frequently conclude partnerships with business and government agencies.

*The entrepreneurial hypotheses maintain their predictive validity in our multivariate analysis. Quite simply, effective leaders exhibit entrepreneurial behavior. More specifically, effective college presidents exhibit entrepreneurial attitudes, values, and behavior. Peck (1983) and others were correct when they hypothesized that successful college presidents behave entrepreneurially. The Kauffman Foundation is correct to emphasize entrepreneurialism as a foundation characteristic of effective leadership, both inside and outside of higher education.*

One might quarrel with the methods by which we derived presidential effectiveness, as Birnbaum (1992) has done. However, we are much more inclined to place confidence in the considered judgment of more than 700 experts from throughout higher education than we are to rely upon the stylized definition of effectiveness proffered by a single individual. Similarly, one might argue that we measure entrepreneurial attitudes, values, and behavior inappropriately. Or one might dispute our sample, or our statistical methods, or our equation specification. Such critiques are appropriate and bound to occur within the free and open marketplace for ideas. Nonetheless, the evidence we have presented here is based upon a large sample, rigorous statistical procedures, numerous control variables, and normative, supportive interviews. It remains for those who do not believe that entrepreneurial attitudes, values, and behavior are important to leadership, or to the American college presidency, to generate their own contributions to this discussion. At this point, we believe the discussion has moved beyond anecdotal presentations, normative speculations, and abstract theorizing and must now focus on empirical verification.

A statistical caveat is in order. While we believe our empirical analysis is both interesting and valid, we would do well to heed the cautions of Friedman and Schwartz (1991), Christ (1993), and Tomek (1993), who warn against reaching strong policy conclusions based upon the statistical significance of coefficients in a single regression equation. We should, they point out, pay more attention to results that are repeatedly confirmed in appropriately rigorous testing circumstances than we do to results, however strong, that emanate from a single study. Leadership is so important a topic that there is a pressing need for additional rigorous, large-sample, controlled empirical work. Yet, of the literally thousands of leadership books that have appeared over the past few decades, only a handful involve any empirical work capable of generalization. This circumstance must change.

## SOME WORDS OF CAUTION

Our results encourage leadership propositions that assert that (1) entrepreneurial presidencies actually exist and their characteristics can be identified, and (2) entrepreneurial presidents tend to be more effective and successful than other presidents. By the same token, our results do not in any sense prove that entrepreneurial approaches to the American college presidency always work, or that they will work for decades on end. Both authors have seen more than a handful of examples of entrepreneurial, transformational presidents who have been egregious failures. Sometimes their entrepreneurial activities are the major cause of their failures. Consider the instructive case of a president of a public university in the west who committed his university and the university's foundation to a significant educational and real estate initiative in another city. The project drew initial praise and had the president's name on it. Information and financial decision making were tightly held. A variety of adverse developments caused the project to go sour well before it was completed, and the resulting financial fallout (a surprise to nearly everyone) was devastating to the university, its foundation, and the president, who was forced to resign. It wasn't that the president's vision in this instance was without merit and possibilities, but the project that resulted was an abject failure, and that failure generated a spate of negative publicity, legislative investigations, adverse coverage in the *Chronicle of Higher Education*, and the end of an otherwise splendid presidential career.

Thus, not everything that has the label *entrepreneurial* on it is meritorious, and not every action that transforms an institution is beneficial. True, the roster of presidential stars is disproportionately filled with entrepreneurial, transformational presidents, but the presidential rogue's gallery also contains a few entrepreneurial presidents. The wise leader must separate the wheat from the chaff with respect to entrepreneurial leadership and fashion her leadership accordingly.

# CHAPTER 7

## Entrepreneurial Examples: The American College Presidency at the Beginning of the Twenty-First Century

A leader is a dealer in hope.

—Napoleon I of France

If a man does not keep pace with his companions, perhaps it is because he hears a different drummer. Let him step to the music he hears, however measured or far away.

—Henry David Thoreau, nineteenth-century American author

Problems are opportunities for those who are astute.

—Anonymous

There is a tendency today for those who write about the college presidency to bemoan the disappearance of the titans among modern American college presidents. Where are the giants, they ask, who used to lead, stimulate, and even dominate American campuses (Ikenberry, 1998)? A particularly thorough survey of this particular genre of lamentations may be found in Crowley's *No Equal in the World* (1994), a marvelous compendium of things (good and bad) that have been said over the years about American college presidents.

Even the popular press has taken interest in the subject, as when the *Washington Post* (Mathews, 2001) asked provocatively, "It's Lowly at the Top: What Became of the Great College Presidents?" Are such presidents ever going to reappear on the academic horizon? The *Post's* Jay Mathews supplied his own answer: "Nah, it's not going to happen. Not even Summers [of Harvard], a genuinely thoughtful man and a big name in Washington, can take us back to those days of superstars in academic robes leading their great faculties into the future. Presidents of other universities say Summers will discover, as they did, that the presidency of even a very famous and selective university is not a bully pulpit but a padded cell" (2001, B01). One can almost hear the music of "Where Have All the Flowers Gone?" floating in the background as a discussion of "shrinking college presidents" proceeds (Greenberg, 1998).

Historically, names such as James Conant and Charles Eliot of Harvard, Robert Hutchins and William Rainey Harper at Chicago, John Hanna at Michigan State, Father Theodore Hesburgh at Notre Dame, Clark Kerr at the University of California, John Silber at Boston University, and Woodrow Wilson at Princeton surged to the fore when powerful, transformational presidents were mentioned. True, more than one of these leaders had powerful enemies, and after long and distinguished service, Clark Kerr ultimately was pushed out by his governing board ("I left the same way I came," he joked, "fired with enthusiasm"), but all were vigorous, visionary leaders who utilized their presidential position as the proverbial bully pulpit and as an implement of change. They were individuals who revitalized their campuses even as they were sought after for their views and as they helped shape the national agenda. These vigorous and influential individuals hardly fit Mathews's deflating assessment of current presidents: "Even PBS bookers ignore them" (2001, B01).

Fisher (1984, 19) has argued that the presidential titans of the past "would not be hired by most boards of trustees today." He may be correct; times have changed, not the least in terms of apparent presidential and governing board agendas. In many cases, potential presidential boat rockers need not apply. Only institutions that perceive themselves to be in crisis seem willing to appoint presidents who clearly and obviously will be change agents. Governing boards often fear change agents; they believe such presidents may harm the institution's fund-raising. Every president today, whether situated in a public or an independent institution, must be an accomplished fund-raiser. Even independent college presidents must be adept politicians, for the prosperity of their institutions sometimes depends upon the whims of legislators, mayors, and city council members as much or more than that of public institutions. Hence, there is less time available for intellectual and social leadership, and there is a tendency for many presidents to shy away from controversial topics.

Gradually, a variety of forces may have narrowed the range of what the public, governing boards, and faculty perceive to be acceptable presidential behavior. Especially in public institutions, there is an increasing tendency for governing boards to specify in great detail what they expect their president to do (and not do). A community college president whom we interviewed commented knowingly, "My board is always looking over my shoulder. They'll corner me at the 7–11, at church, at the Lions, everywhere. They think they represent the public interest and should run this place [the community college]." While most college presidents today are not myrmidons, blindly following detailed orders from their governing boards, the smaller and more localized the institution, and the more shaky its financial circumstances, the more likely it is that the institution's governing board will place a heavy hand on the president and become involved in micromanagement, the dreaded term that presidents customarily apply to circumstances involving what they believe to be inappropriate governing board interference.

Nonetheless, all is not lost. In the preceding chapters, we introduced strong evidence in favor of the notion that many presidents can and do make major differences in their institutions. Quite simply, some presidents are more effective than others, and our evidence helps us to understand why. However, to lend emphasis to this point, in the second part of this chapter, we provide the reader with 17 profiles of especially successful, effective, entrepreneurial presidents. Such individuals exist in all sectors of higher education and should be recognized and praised.

*We have found considerable overlap between the effective presidents and the entrepreneurial presidents. In fact, the entrepreneurial character of many presidents usually is the mainspring of their success, though on occasion it can be their downfall.* Entrepreneurial presidents are flexible, innovative, and especially capable of perceiving relationships and opportunities that ordinary presidents do not. They leverage resources, negotiate groundbreaking partnerships, turn their organizations in new directions, and clearly take risks, albeit well-calculated risks. They are more likely to develop ad hoc structures to accomplish their goals, are not afraid to violate the status quo, and personally generate many innovative ideas. In most circumstances, their institutions are better off because of their leadership. Far from a situation of not making a difference, the prototype effective entrepreneurial president is a pulsating energy source who transforms her campus.

Do all campuses need a transformational, entrepreneurial president at all points in time? Perhaps not. Conditions and needs on American campuses vary, and in some cases a transactional, representative president may be what the doctor ordered, at least in the short term. Over the long term, however, most institutions cannot afford to sit still. Campus constituents, especially those who enjoy perquisites and have reason to fear change, may enjoy the era of good feelings and apparent security engendered by many transactional, representative presidencies. Nonetheless, these circumstances tend to degenerate over time, and crises often arise, sometimes unexpectedly, because of institutional torpor. At that juncture, the transactional, representative president often is befuddled, accustomed to languor, and not knowing where to turn.

Thus, the absence of transformational, entrepreneurial campus leadership has a disturbing tendency to lead to institutional expenses exceeding revenues, curricula that are stale and out of date, fund-raising that is laggard, and physical plants that gradually deteriorate. Often, these trends go unnoticed by the campus or the governing board until they have accelerated to dangerous levels. Unfortunately, we have observed this general institutional pattern and its variants altogether more frequently than is necessary.

Well, then, how does a campus become "hot"? How does a campus reinvigorate itself? How can colleges and universities transform their circumstances and achieve goals that many previously thought impossible? Leadership—transformational, effective, and entrepreneurial—is an important (probably the most important) element. We invite you to study the following success stories involving 17 highly successful, sitting American college presidents. These presidents toil at both public and independent institutions; they are located at both two-year and four-year colleges; their institutions are both small and large; some of their institutions are religiously affiliated; the missions and histories of their institutions differ substantially; some lead research institutions, while others lead liberal arts colleges; these presidents include both women and men; they include both minorities and Caucasians; they are located in all sections of the United States. What they have in common, however, is conspicuous presidential success. Their examples demonstrate the transforming possibilities of effective, entrepreneurial presidencies and provide a sense of realism to the general empirical analysis that we have presented in the previous three chapters.

## RITA BORNSTEIN, ROLLINS COLLEGE

When Rita Bornstein was elected president of Rollins College in 1990, it was a good institution with great ambitions, but scant resources and an aging physical plant. To transform the college from good to great, she focused on strengthening the school's quality, reputation, and financial health. Her vision for Rollins was that it be recognized as one of the top colleges in the nation. She has attained that goal, as Rollins ranked second among all master's level institutions in the South in the 2003 *U.S. News and World Report* rankings.

Ms. Bornstein brought to the presidency considerable leadership experience and had presided over several large-scale institutional change efforts. She led a transformation at Rollins that began with raising standards in all areas, selectively expanding the membership and improving the functioning of the board of trustees, enhancing the efficiency and effectiveness of the administration, making more rigorous the process and criteria for faculty evaluation, and increasing selectivity in admissions. Tangible results of the efforts included increased student applications, enrollment, and quality; recruitment of top-quality faculty, staff, and trustees; campus beautification and expansion; successful commercial ventures; and financial stability.

Early in the 1990s, President Bornstein mounted *The Campaign for Rollins*, with an ambitious goal of $100 million. Despite the depressed economy, decline in student enrollment, budget deficits, and downsizing that characterized the period, Bornstein forged ahead and raised an unprecedented $160.2 million. This helped provide the resources needed to transform the college. Fifteen new endowed chairs were established, new academic and student-development programs launched, financial aid funds increased, new centers and institutes created, six buildings renovated or added, and a spectacular entrance gateway created. Almost half of the funds raised went to the endowment, which quadrupled in value. A $10 million endowment raised to support the presidency was the first in the nation.

According to Charles E. Rice, the former chair of Rollins' board of trustees, "Rita's untiring dedication to Rollins and commitment to excellence have propelled the College to new academic heights, as acknowledged by the College's national rankings and reputation." Frank H. Barker, subsequent board chairman, added that "her exceptionally strong commitment to quality" has led "to the transformation of Rollins as a nationally recognized institution. Her mark is evident in all aspects of the College." Unquestionably, she is a president who has made a profound difference in her institution.

## SALLY CLAUSEN, PRESIDENT, UNIVERSITY OF LOUISIANA SYSTEM

"Dr. Sally Clausen is recognized throughout the state and nation as a dynamic, innovative leader in higher education. Few people are so competent and qualified to lead colleges and universities." So said the *Natchitoches Times* on September 14, 2002. Her board chair, Gordon Pugh, wrote, "Sally Clausen has been the most effective spokesperson that I have seen in any organization." Board member Andre Coudrain, the chair of her evaluation committee, described her performance as "off the charts." Board member Carroll Suggs said, "She has no peers." And so the plaudits come from each campus in the University of Louisiana System as well as from the governor's office. Sally Clausen defines what a system head should be.

It is perhaps not coincidental that before heading a system, Dr. Clausen was a campus president at Southeastern Louisiana University in the heart of David Duke country; 15,000 students, 94 percent white. Improving diversity became her calling card. She appointed an African American female as her assistant. She attended churches in the African American community and welcomed African American ministers and their spouses into her home. She held public forums on diversity (one of which won a national award), and she dealt directly with fraternity students and their influential alumni regarding a Confederate battle flag that hung proudly on their front lawn. After considerable dialogue, the president of the fraternity removed the flag and publicly thanked her for her interest and support. She traveled to Europe and Latin America to establish exchange programs for faculty and students and raised private scholarship money to help them with travel expenses. Results were impressive: a 58 percent increase in African American enrollment, a 24 percent increase in students from other countries, and a 62 percent increase in travel abroad opportunities.

During this productive time, faculty salaries at Southeast increased by 22 percent in four years, Dr. Clausen convinced legislators to increase the institution's operating budget by 52 percent, and she gained approval for $70 million of state-of-the-art academic and student facilities. She, along with university and community representatives, developed an enlightened strategic plan, admission standards were raised, private funding increased, and partnerships were established with the public schools and the business community.

It was those qualities that the Board of Supervisors cited when they asked her to accept the position of system president to lead eight regional universities enrolling over 80,000 students. The system was in need of strong leadership. Two of its eight universities (ULM, the University of Louisiana at Monroe and GSU, Grambling State University) had received audit disclaimers from the State Legislative Auditor. Both universities were sanctioned by the Southern Association of Colleges and Schools (SACS). Severe and sustained enrollment declines and turnover in key personnel were major contributors to the negative audits and required stabilization. The media and legislators were questioning the board's appointments of presidents and its ability to manage its institutions.

A corrective action plan was quickly developed for both universities, involving several facets: Dr. Clausen commissioned institutional reviews of each university, which led to action and realistic strategic planning. Leadership changes occurred at both institutions—at the president and vice president levels at ULM, and an experienced new chief financial officer at GSU. Dramatic personnel changes were made that resulted in terminating more than 130 staff at Grambling (it was the largest single termination in the history of the state).

Dr. Clausen also delivered a clear, yet diplomatic message to legislators and to the governor's office—"You will be respectfully informed of university progress, but you must stay out of university business and personnel actions." This was not an easy message to deliver (especially since her budget derived from both) but, as an important African American legislator commented, "She was firm but so sincere that I felt Grambling was in good hands and I would help her by getting out of her way." Former Speaker of the House, Representative Hunt Downer, observed, "She is the best and most effective leader I have ever observed; no one inspires more confidence or respect, so if she says something, just sit back and watch the show."

Eighteen months later, the results were swift and impressive. The Legislative Auditor, citing phenomenal progress and complimenting new leadership at both ULM and the system office, issued an unqualified opinion on the 2002 financial statements. SACS lifted the sanction at ULM shortly thereafter. During that same period of time, the Legislative Auditor issued an "unqualified opinion" on Grambling's financial statements for the first time in four years, and a few months late, SACS continued the university's accreditation and noted "significant positive change at the University of Louisiana System and at Grambling."

In a time when the chief executive officers of state higher education systems are frequently criticized as inept, Sally Clausen has established the model for competence and achievement in that arena.

## WILLIAM R. HARVEY, HAMPTON UNIVERSITY

Hampton Institute—Hampton University since 1984—was founded in 1868 to educate young African Americans to "go out to teach and lead their people." Under the exceptional leadership of President William R. Harvey, it has become an exceedingly successful institution that not only is acknowledged as one of the half dozen best historically Black colleges and universities (HBCUs), but also is seen as a legitimate, powerful player among all institutions nationally. Many regard Bill Harvey, who unquestionably is a strong, visionary, and highly energetic leader, as the very best

HBCU president in America—no mean distinction in a field that numbers more than 100.

When Dr. Harvey arrived at Hampton in 1978, the institution was experiencing endemic financial deficits. The institution has never had a deficit since then and has sextupled its endowment, which now stands at $165 million, trailing only Howard and Spelman among HBCUs. Hampton raised $264 million in its most recent capital campaign.

Meanwhile, Hampton's attractive waterside campus has been transformed with more than a dozen new buildings, many of which were funded by gifts from corporations such as Scripps Howard. Dr. Harvey is a past master at attracting influential individuals to the Hampton Board of Trustees, including individuals ranging from actress Elizabeth Taylor to Roger Enrico, the president of Pepsi-Cola. He develops intriguing partnerships with governmental agencies and fearlessly uses these partnerships as the fulcrum to expand Hampton's curriculum, which now includes doctoral programs in physics and pharmacy.

Bill Harvey is an indefatigable exponent of Hampton and has used a variety of means to promote the institution, including the fine arts and intercollegiate athletics. Hampton joined the NCAA's Division I only in 1995, but a few years later already was defeating the likes of nationally ranked Iowa State in the men's NCAA basketball tournament. Bill Harvey seldom pushes Hampton in any direction without an expectation of nationally legitimate success.

Dr. Harvey's willingness to mentor those reporting to him has resulted in nine individuals moving from Hampton to the presidencies of other institutions of higher education. His model of administration is not one that all adore, for he is a strong, determined leader who does not easily tolerate individuals with lesser levels of energy and commitment. But all agree that Hampton University is immeasurably better off in 2004 than it was in 1978 when Bill Harvey assumed the presidential helm. His name and the name of Hampton University now are almost synonymous; it is not surprising that both political parties in Virginia are rumored to be courting him as a possible statewide political candidate.

How has he accomplished these amazing feats? Dr. Harvey has invested himself totally in Hampton University. He has never been reluctant to approach the Caucasian power structure and to demonstrate to corporations how they can simultaneously meet their own goals and make a huge difference at Hampton. Further, he has held his faculty and students to externally validated national standards. Hampton University is an HBCU and justifiably proud of its heritage, but its expectations, goals, and performance standards reflect President Harvey's insistence that Hampton can and will compete with any institution.

On any list of outstanding, transformational presidents, Bill Harvey of Hampton University must occupy a prime position. What he has accomplished in the face of steep odds might well be labeled amazing.

## JACK HAWKINS, JR., TROY STATE UNIVERSITY

Jack Hawkins, Jr., chancellor of Troy State University (TSU), describes effective leadership this way: "The most important thing is to hire good people and get out of their way. Don't micromanage and don't look over their shoulders, but hold their feet to the fire to perform effectively. The goal is, always serve the students first."

This approach has served Hawkins well since he became chancellor of the Troy State University System in 1989. He took over a system that needed a renaissance. And reborn it was. Today, through University College, which receives no state funding, Troy offers degree programs at more than 50 military installations and metropolitan locations in 14 U.S. states and seven foreign nations, and it operates two independently accredited universities: TSU Montgomery and TSU Dothan. Administrative control of the Troy System is headquartered on the main campus. At this writing, TSU is expanding its operations in the Pacific, recently opened an office in Malaysia, and is planning sites for Vietnam and Thailand. Over the last decade, the number of nations represented in the Troy student body has grown from 13 to 62.

At the same time, more than $65 million has been invested in system facilities, both renovation and new construction, enrollment increased from 14,000 students to more than 22,000 today, and grants and contracts grew from less than $250,000 to more than $10 million annually.

Operating a worldwide institution is not without problems. Maintaining standards across the board was a challenge. This was underscored in 1993 when the visiting team of the Commission on Colleges, Southern Association of Colleges and Schools (SACS), issued approximately 125 recommendations during its reaffirmation of accreditation visit. The most recent SACS visit resulted in only 13 recommendations, plus two commendations.

In a further effort to maintain standards, Hawkins is consolidating the three independent campuses of the system. The plan will serve students by removing barriers created by independent accreditation, which restrict the transfer of courses between campuses. It will achieve greater efficiency by eliminating duplication in administrative and academic matters. TSU will create one faculty handbook, one course catalog, one academic calendar for all campuses and will also eliminate confusion by instituting uniform policies and procedures—such as common course numbers and names. The merger is predicted to save $16 million over the next decade. Uniform policies and standards will be applied from Troy to Montgomery to Hong Kong to the Internet, where TSU enrolls more than 3,000 students.

Hawkins says, "Our vision for the future is weighed toward using a combination of traditional methods and distance-learning methods to serve the greatest number of students in the most efficient manner."

Troy State is the story of an energetic leader and an institution accurately measuring the market and then responding quickly and accurately to the signals they received. Tens of thousands of students, often situated in unconventional and distant locations, owe their access to higher education to Jack Hawkins and Troy State. Dr. Hawkins found a highly productive niche in higher education and demonstrated once again how leadership makes a difference.

## FREEMAN A. HRABOWSKI, UNIVERSITY OF MARYLAND, BALTIMORE COUNTY (UMBC)

In spring of 1987, Freeman Hrabowski was walking into the Administration Building and encountered hundreds of African American student protesters. A staff member assured him there was no cause for concern. "Don't worry," she said. "This happens every spring." His first thought was that the last time he had seen a Black-student protest was at Hampton University in the sixties, and he had participated; his second thought was that, ironically, he had now become "The Administration."

Sixteen years have passed since his startling introduction to UMBC, and he is now in his eleventh year as president there. During that time, the climate on the campus has shifted from one that routinely included protests to one that celebrates high achievement among students, including African Americans. With approximately 12,000 students and increasingly selective admissions, UMBC enjoys a diverse student body (one-third minority), and the campus focuses especially upon providing research opportunities and internships for undergraduates.

To create a supportive environment for minority students, Hrabowski convinced colleagues to strengthen support for *all* students. He led the campus through an intensive self-examination involving students, department chairs, faculty, and staff. These efforts produced solutions ranging from encouraging group study to enhancing the freshman experience. Within this broader context, the campus also focused on creating a more positive climate for minority students. His vision—inspired by both UMBC's research mission and the nationwide paucity of minorities in science—was to create a cadre of superbly educated minority students who would become leading research scientists.

The result was the creation in 1988 of the Meyerhoff Scholars Program (named for Baltimore philanthropist Robert Meyerhoff) for high-achieving minority students in science and engineering. The program is now a national model, and due to its extraordinary success, Hrabowski's university was among the first recipients of the U.S. Presidential Award for Excellence in Science, Mathematics, and Engineering Mentoring (1996). To date, the program has produced more than 330 graduates, 85 percent of whom have gone on to graduate and professional school.

Hrabowski also gave considerable attention to expanding research productivity, building the university's infrastructure, increasing its endowment, expanding its role in economic development and public service, and raising its national visibility. Named by *Newsweek* one of the nation's twelve "Hot Schools" in 2003, UMBC is a research-extensive institution, according to the Carnegie Foundation. It has added more than $300 million of new facilities, has far exceeded its capital campaign goals, and is the nation's intercollegiate chess champion. UMBC's ubiquitous president is constantly on the move, speaking to students, educators, policymakers, and a wide range of professional groups nationwide about education. He epitomizes the transformational president.

## STEPHEN M. JORDAN, EASTERN WASHINGTON UNIVERSITY

When Stephen M. Jordan became president of Eastern Washington University in 1998, the university had just endured five years of declining enrollments, barely escaped being merged into another institution, been chastised by the state legislature, and experienced plummeting faculty and staff morale. Jordan's first step was to break with the tradition of recent presidents, who lived in private homes in nearby Spokane. Instead, he moved into the former President's Home on campus. Students were encouraged to stop by. He was visible everywhere, including the campus bookstore, where he personally apologized to waiting parents and incoming freshmen when the store opened late one fall morning. He and his wife went for walks in the surrounding community and got to know the neighbors.

He quickly tackled problems. At his first all-campus address, he stated unflinchingly that the university could not afford to do all that it had done historically and that some programs would have to be eliminated. He made the recruitment of new, residential freshmen a strong focus. The university's niche would be career preparation underpinned by a strong liberal arts base. Further, Eastern would partner with regional business and industry in applied research.

In four years, enrollment increased by 25 percent, the campus infrastructure improved dramatically, new programs were added, partnerships with other universities and community colleges were established, and a major capital campaign was initiated.

All agree that under Steve Jordan's leadership, Eastern Washington University is now considered to be a player in the state of Washington and an economic driver in the eastern part of the state. It is remarkable that all of this was generated from the depths of despair in a period of less than five years.

## MARIE V. MCDEMMOND, NORFOLK STATE UNIVERSITY

Since becoming president of Norfolk State University (NSU) in July 1997, Marie V. McDemmond has transformed challenges into opportunities. And this has been accomplished against formidable odds, both substantive and psychological. Upon arrival Dr. McDemmond faced a projected $6.5 million state operating deficit and an auxiliary deficit of over $4.7 million. NSU Athletics alone had a deficit of $2.5 million as the university began its first year in Division I competition. Nor was her appointment popular with the long-established institutional hierarchy.

President McDemmond negotiated a five-year, no-interest state loan (repaid within two and a half years). She accomplished this, obtained reaffirmation by SACS, and created a university-wide participatory budget and planning process, all within her first year. She reduced academic schools from nine to five and cut operating expenditures by $4 million.

McDemmond also led efforts to secure additional state resources. Timing was critical due to the pending resolution of Virginia's long-standing accord with the U.S. Office of Civil Rights, an outcome of the *Adams* and *Fordice* cases. Her efforts resulted in greatly enhanced funding for such critical issues as Y2K compliance, student technology access, and the creation of specific academic niches to attract a diverse, quality student body.

In her first five years, state funding to NSU increased over 56.7 percent, in spite of declining state revenues. In anticipation of reduced base funding, McDemmond instituted an early retirement plan, ultimately accepted by 27 senior faculty, that provided a pool of funds to provide institutional flexibility.

While the university historically had functioned as an open admissions institution, Virginia's expanded accountability measures placed NSU at the bottom of its peers in such critical measures as retention and graduation rates. McDemmond raised admissions standards and at the same time made improvements to academic programs and advising to insure student success. Enrollments, which previously had declined to less than 7,000, began to rise again. The admissions profile of NSU's most recent freshman class shows a gain of 11.5 percent in GPA scores and 12.2 percent in SAT scores. After five years, the freshmen retention rate has improved by almost 11 percent, and NSU's graduation rate has increased by 35 percent. Another critical measure—the federal government student loan default rate—has been reduced from 27 percent to 6 percent.

Internal reallocations and market salary adjustments for faculty provided funding for new program initiatives, such as niche-focused distance learning programs and transfer programs with community colleges. Research and sponsored programs funding increased over 42.9 percent since 2000.

McDemmond also expanded the university's fund-raising arm and initiated new marketing strategies to give the university a carefully focused image, resulting in an increase of 87 percent in annual fund giving and 219.6 percent in alumni giving since 2000. A comprehensive campaign is on the drawing board, as well as a public/private partnership to develop a research and corporate park, additional residence halls, a renovation and expansion to the student center, and the renovation of three academic buildings.

## IRVING PRESSLEY MCPHAIL, COMMUNITY COLLEGE OF BALTIMORE COUNTY, MARYLAND

Irving Pressley McPhail has led CCBC to a phoenix-like renewal. He inherited a plethora of problems, including the growing pains of a complicated reorganization. CCBC was "in chaos" according to an outside institutional review because of declining enrollment, documented leadership failures, the absence of a clear mission, and atrocious morale problems. CCBC was still operating as a system of three independent, often competing branches.

Chancellor McPhail has pursued an unwavering focus on student learning. He rallied faculty and staff to create an institution where student learning was first and foremost in every aspect of the college's operations. The college's integrated planning process ties all budget-making and resource decisions to the mission of improving student learning.

The result has been a kaleidoscope of achievement that has garnered national awards and recognition. In virtually every area that counts, CCBC is light-years ahead of where it was before McPhail arrived. Enrollment is up; relations with trustees and public officials are restored; the college has infused technology in and out of the classroom; it has developed a significant presence in online course delivery; it has developed a reputation for sound budgeting and financial management; it has attracted committed new faculty and invigorated veteran faculty with competitive merit salaries; and it launched an impressive Closing the Gap initiative that concentrates upon bridging the black/white learning divide. Amid all this, relations with trustees and public officials are on solid ground, and morale is vastly improved.

McPhail has been the catalyst for change at an institution that had been floundering. Essentially, he persuaded three formerly independent institutions to renew themselves and to meet the challenges and opportunities of the twenty-first century. CCBC's new centralized focus and remarkable renaissance provides valuable lessons for many other struggling, albeit promising institutions.

## SCOTT D. MILLER, WESLEY COLLEGE

"Wesley Works Wonders" trumpeted the front-page headline of a March 2003 issue of *State News Sunday*, Dover, Delaware's daily newspaper. The subtitle read, "It's Miller time." Less than six years earlier, banners in the region's papers had proclaimed doom for the 130-year-old United Methodist Church–affiliated liberal arts college, culminating in a July 1997 headline proclaiming "Troubled Wesley Names New President."

Scott D. Miller, then just 38, but already possessing seven years of presidential experience, took this challenge and launched an extensive restructuring process. He developed an agenda to innovate, lead and plan strategically, solve problems, create efficient financial structures, and operate with fiscal responsibility. He proceeded to involve students, faculty, staff, alumni, and the Board of Trustees in transforming Delaware's oldest college.

After his appointment, but before his arrival, Dr. Miller and the Board of Trustees commissioned a comprehensive institutional review (using a prominent group of national experts) that examined all aspects of campus operations and helped craft the college's blueprint for the future. The review resulted in a 128-page working document with 60 rather specific recommendations for change.

Under Miller's leadership, Wesley's applications tripled, and enrollment more than doubled to 2,300. The SAT scores of incoming freshmen rose by 133 points, and the retention rate increased to a consistent 90 percent from 52 percent. A decade of budget deficits was eliminated and the budget balanced every year while overall revenues tripled. In addition, President Miller renewed and improved a sagging relationship between Wesley and the Methodist Church, engineered vast improvements in business practices, privatized some campus housing, eliminated a long-standing censure of the institution by the AAUP, and raised almost $50 million, earning raves from the Council for the Advancement and Support of Education.

By any standard, this is an impressive story involving a leader who turned an institution around and led it to prosperity.

## CONSTANTINE PAPADAKIS, DREXEL UNIVERSITY

In 1995, Drexel University was suffering from a decade of almost continuous decline. Student headcount had decreased by 50 percent, and the institution had reduced its workforce and frozen salaries. An estimated $87 million in much-needed maintenance and infrastructure improvement had been deferred. Key assets were sold off. The institution was approaching a crisis.

Enter Constantine Papadakis, formerly the dean of engineering at the University of Cincinnati. Papadakis brought his signature approach—bold, high-energy, business-oriented leadership—to the task of rebuilding Drexel. His first priority was to address an administrative culture that had contributed to Drexel's failures. To that end, he replaced more than 130 administrators in his first months. Every university vice president except one was "graduated," as Papadakis put it, and he set about building a solid, innovative management team that would look to the future.

Papadakis focused on Drexel's core strengths. Founded during the Industrial Revolution to prepare young men and women for new technologies, Drexel had been a technological leader. The university boasted the nation's second-largest co-op program, and the institution's urban Philadelphia location is such a rich resource that Papadakis took to calling it Drexel's "living laboratory." Papadakis concentrated upon these positives.

A back-to-basics approach helped sell Drexel to prospective students. By 2002, undergraduate applications had tripled, and full-time undergraduate enrollment had nearly doubled. The average SAT score of incoming freshmen rose more than 100 points.

As the student body improved, so did the faculty, creating what Papadakis called a "circle of quality"—stronger faculty attract stronger students, and more accomplished students attract stronger faculty. Drexel faculty members brought more than $105 million in contract and grant awards to the university in 2001 and 2002, while research expenditures in the same year climbed to $41 million, compared with $14 million four years earlier.

In 1995, Drexel's Standard & Poor's bond rating was below investment grade. Since then, the university has been upgraded three times, and it now claims an "A" rating. Drexel's success has led to increased external support. It raised $204 million between 1998 and 2002, compared with $67 million in the previous five-year period. In the eight years from 1995 to 2003, the university's endowment grew from $90 million to $350 million even while it invested $150 million in capital improvements.

In 1998, Drexel daringly agreed to operate and eventually acquire the bankrupt Allegheny University of the Health Sciences, a good academic institution nearly destroyed by mismanagement. The risk was great, but the opportunity was even greater. The turnaround was remarkable. More than 14,000 related jobs were preserved. The Drexel University College of Medicine, the nation's largest private school of medicine, broke even in 2002, less than four years removed from bankruptcy. The consolidation of the two institutions in July 2002 created a university with 5,300 employees and 16,500 students.

Nationally, when entrepreneurial presidents are cited, the name of Constantine Papadakis surges to the fore. His striking success is remarkable.

## GEORGE A. PRUITT, THOMAS EDISON STATE COLLEGE

George Pruitt has served as president of New Jersey's Edison State College since 1982. The college has pioneered methods in distance education, the assessment of prior learning, and adult-centered higher education. These niches remain, and the college's annual National Institute for Prior Learning attracts practitioners from all over the country. Under Pruitt's leadership, the college became one of the first institutions in the country to offer an external Bachelor of Science in Nursing degree, and it also began to develop its own extended course, examination, and program offerings in all academic areas. Today, Edison's Center for Distance and Independent Adult Learning (DIAL) offers 200 distance-delivered courses to 5,000 students. An online Master of Science in Management degree program was inaugurated in 1997, and a Master of Arts in Professional Studies program followed in 2000. Edison's enrollment has tripled, and the number of degree programs has doubled.

As enrollment and programs grew, the college built a campus in the Capitol District in the City of Trenton. In 1999, the college took possession of a newly renovated space comprising three historic townhouses adjoining its original building. These townhouses were painstakingly restored, and although they are on the National Register of Historic Places, they house state-of-the-art distance learning equipment.

Under Pruitt's direction, the college formed partnerships to serve new populations at a distance through the eArmy University, the Navy College Partners program, and the University of South Africa. Today, the college is well recognized as a leader in distance-delivered education. *Forbes Magazine* has identified the college as among the top 20 colleges in the country in the use of technology to create distance learning opportunities.

Throughout all of these changes, changes that have brought the college from relative obscurity to frequent recognition, Pruitt has remained faithful to the college's distinctive mission and values. But he also served as chairman of the board of the Chamber of Commerce, a director of two banks, and a member of the boards of three universities, two hospitals, two economic development organizations, and several national education associations. For good reason, many label George Pruitt "the president's president."

## EARL RICHARDSON, MORGAN STATE UNIVERSITY

Morgan State University in Baltimore stands as a striking example of presidential leadership. When Earl Richardson became president in 1984, the very life of the university was in jeopardy. He found an institution with declining enrollment, limited programs, a demoralized faculty (many with marginal qualifications), a deteriorating physical plant, and reduced state support. Add to this daunting condition the reality that his appointment was not warmly welcomed by the broader community or by the campus. Many thought he was appointed to hasten Morgan's decline. They did not know Earl Richardson. Today, virtually all in the state, the region, and beyond have great respect for President Richardson, and on campus he is a hero.

One of the first actions taken by Richardson was the highly unpopular one of reducing the size of Morgan's faculty by some 70 positions in order to align staffing levels with enrollments. More than one-third of those faculty terminated were tenured. Few college presidents would have survived such a retrenchment of tenured faculty, but Richardson crafted a five-year severance pay package for those affected. He also moved aggressively to initiate and develop academic programs with potential for enrollment growth, including engineering, information systems management, telecommunications, and architecture, all of which are now accredited. Significant reallocations of staff and budgets were required to develop these additional programs, for which the state initially provided no additional funding.

While operating funds from the state were limited, Richardson was able to convince the state to fund through general obligation bonds a major program of renovation and new construction that continues today. During the past 15 years, projects totaling over $250 million have virtually rebuilt the campus; over $200 million is programmed for the future.

Campus enrollments are now at an all-time high. The faculty is well credentialed. Morgan now ranks among the leading campuses nationally in the number of degrees awarded to African Americans overall, as well as ranking high in key fields such as engineering, biological sciences, and business. It ranks first nationally in electrical engineering and near the top in civil and industrial engineering. Due to the productivity of Morgan's engineering programs, Maryland may be unique among states in that African Americans now receive engineering degrees at about the same rate at which they receive bachelor's degrees generally. The university is now about to have the same impact on African Americans receiving doctoral degrees. Morgan has already increased the number of African Americans receiving doctorates in the state by about 50 percent.

Though facing obstacles at virtually every point, Earl Richardson possessed a vision that he conveyed with passion, charm, intelligence, and persistence. Today, Dr. Richardson and Morgan State stand admired by all.

## RICHARD RIDENOUR, MARIAN COLLEGE, WISCONSIN

Physician/psychiatrist, medical educator, leader, and retired Navy Rear Admiral (two stars), Richard Ridenour, M.D., came to Marian College from the command of "The President's Hospital" (the National Naval Medical Center in Bethesda, Maryland). As a non-Catholic with a military background, Dick Ridenour didn't think he would be seriously considered for the presidency, but he thought the process could be fun and useful. It was, and to the ultimate pleasure of all, he was appointed.

In six years, the transformation at Marian has been nothing short of astonishing. He entered the presidency during a time of steadily declining student numbers and financial hardship at the college. Opening the books and laying the finances of the institution on the table, he convinced the faculty to support a one-year wage freeze. He appointed officers, trusted and empowered them, and held them and himself accountable. The mission statement was refined, a vision was shaped, an outside institutional assessment was conducted, and a realistic strategic plan was developed. Today, they are a happy and remarkably productive team with an experienced captain at the helm.

He and fellow board members re-energized and renewed the membership of the Board of Trustees, which today includes major corporate CEOs, international representatives, important local community and area voices, and a strong church membership.

In five years, the college's endowment and invested funds increased 10 times. How? Ridenour secured an unusual grant of nearly $1 million to build and sustain a highly professional advancement staff. He appointed a top development officer, and fund-raising soared. Marian exceeded its $16 million capital campaign goal, the largest in the school's and the area's history. In six years, over $38 million was raised. The college also completed construction of both a $1.2 million Alumni Center and a $12 million Center for Technology and Executive Learning, the first new major construction projects in over 15 years.

Reflecting the needs of society, the college became a recognized leader in the state of Wisconsin in the area of diversity. A Center for Spirituality & Leadership was created. A series of innovative, highly marketable new academic programs were developed, including an Honors Program, a dual-track Master's in Nursing program, an Applied Information Technology (AIT) program, an Interdisciplinary Studies program, and a series of articulation agreements with Wisconsin's technical colleges and the U.S. Marshals Service. Then Marian secured funds to complete an extensive information technology plan, wire every campus building, provide up-to-date workstations for students, faculty, and staff, and connect multiple distant campuses.

The face of the campus has changed dramatically: the grounds were beautified, new signage and campus external lighting were installed, residence halls were renovated, an athletic complex developed, and the student center was restructured. All of this has been achieved in fiscal circumstances that many would regard as Spartan. Dr. Ridenour secured gifts, created partnerships, and inspired constituents and friends to believe in the future of the college and the value of its mission.

The chief campus cheerleader, Dick Ridenour also led a dramatic change in campus culture, first evidenced by the creation of a Spirit Flag, which now seems present everywhere, and then by an obvious increase in the wearing of clothing with the Marian College logo, and finally by creating a highly popular set of cultural and sporting events. One rarely finds President Ridenour roaming the campus without his Marian College baseball hat. If he's not wearing it, students quickly let him know something's wrong!

Perhaps the hallmark of the Admiral's entrepreneurial spirit can be seen in the unique special programs of opportunity for education and life change that he has helped create and fund. These include the Excel program, which helps previously underperforming students earn a college opportunity and later succeed. The college also has pioneered its Working Families program, which allows single parents to become full-time students by giving them a unique offering of tuition support, social and professional support, childcare support, food, and housing aid. A stringent GPA requirement applies, and there is a four-year graduation demand and a significant community service component. It's a one-of-a-kind program.

Students have found the college's rebirth very attractive. Traditional student applications increased 45 percent and total enrollment 24 percent. The academic qualifications of the freshmen class have improved, even while the number of minority students increased 65 percent. Faculty also have found the Marian renaissance enticing. The percentage of faculty with terminal degrees has risen from 47 percent to 64 percent and, for the first time ever at Marian College, several endowed chairs have been created.

The academic excellence and the contributions of Marian College to its greater community are no longer secrets in the upper Midwest region. Neither is the pride that students, staff, and faculty evince for their college. Admiral Ridenour has demonstrated that leadership can transform even those institutions that are small in size and whose demographic and financial environments are weak. Today, none would dispute that Dick Ridenour is the spirit of Marian College.

## STEVEN B. SAMPLE, UNIVERSITY OF SOUTHERN CALIFORNIA

Widely regarded as one of the best university presidents of his generation, Dr. Steven B. Sample has propelled the University of Southern California (USC) into the top tier of American research universities. Yet he did not inherit this distinction. In 1991, when Sample was inaugurated as USC's tenth president, the university faced problems in a number of areas. Financially, the university was struggling with budget deficits and massive layoffs, due in part to the fact that California's economy was mired in a deep recession. Academically, while USC's graduate and professional programs were highly regarded around the country, its undergraduate program was not. The university was accepting applications for the fall as late as one week into the semester, and it was not attracting its share of the nation's top students. USC's dropout rates were high, while its graduation rates were abysmally low.

Soon after he arrived at USC, Sample helped the university clarify its vision by drafting a concise role and mission statement and leading the effort to formulate a highly focused strategic plan. Sample considers USC's role and mission statement and its strategic plan to be among the most valuable documents the university possesses because they have been widely read and internalized by trustees, faculty, staff, and other constituents.

Sample helped solve USC's financial troubles by proving his gifts as a fund-raiser. Indeed, the *Los Angeles Times* recently hailed him as "perhaps the most successful fund-raising president of all time." Sample is the only university president ever to secure four gifts of $100 million or more. Under Sample's leadership, USC more than quadrupled its endowment (to $2.2 billion) over a 10-year period. In 2002, USC surpassed Harvard as the most successful fund-raising university in a single year by raising more than $585 million in cash gifts and private support. Recently, USC completed the most successful fundraising campaign in the history of higher education, raising nearly $2.9 billion during its nine-year Building on Excellence campaign.

Known as a compelling motivator with an understated, yet inspirational style, Sample also has transformed USC's academic programs. The mean SAT score of admitted students is now 1335, an increase of 265 points during his tenure. USC is now one of the most academically selective universities in the nation, receiving 11 applicants for every opening in the freshman class.

Today's USC is a stark contrast to the 1991 version. Sample's bold and compelling leadership has transformed USC in every area and has vaulted the university into the very top ranks of American research universities. USC is one of only five major research universities to be designated as Leadership Institutions by the Association of American Colleges and Universities for the excellence of its undergraduate programs. The university has nearly doubled its sponsored research funding and now ranks ninth among all private universities in terms of the dollar volume of federal research support. During Sample's tenure, USC has nearly doubled the number of faculty who have been elected to membership in the three major national academies, and faculty member George Olah was awarded the Nobel Prize in Chemistry for work he did at USC. *Time Magazine/Princeton Review* named USC its College of the Year in 2000 for its culture of public service and community outreach. In its 2001 guide to colleges,

*Newsweek-Kaplan* named USC a "hot school" because of its success in attracting the very best students.

Steven Sample is considered by many experts to be the single most effective college president in the United States. He provides a particularly vivid example of how presidential leadership makes the difference.

## KENNETH A. SHAW, SYRACUSE UNIVERSITY

In 1991, Syracuse University was facing the double bind of a demographic dip in the number of typical college-going 18-year-olds and a worsening economy. Enrollment had dropped, and the number of students needing significant financial aid had increased. The institution faced an annual deficit of approximately $40 million. Kenneth "Buzz" Shaw assumed the presidency in August of that year.

Prior to his appointment, he had gently but markedly transformed two university systems, the University of Wisconsin and Southern Illinois University. Indeed, his entire career in Illinois, Maryland, and New York had been one of dramatically improving conditions without undue conflict. In Maryland, at Towson University, he was known as the "self-actualizing change agent." When he left after eight years, the substance and spirit of the university had turned around completely, and he was widely loved.

At Syracuse, he met with representative groups prior to his arrival in an effort to identify a consensus on the most pressing issues. Shaw acknowledged that the campus was bound to grieve the old ways of doing things, even while he urged the university community to move forward as quickly as possible. He reminded people of the institution's mission and core values and challenged them to think of a new vision for the future.

He stressed that even though budget considerations were paramount and cuts inevitable, the essence of the university and its unique strengths must be not only preserved, but also enhanced. The many events planned to introduce him to the campus and wider communities became occasions for him to stress the core values and mission and to reinforce his intention to make only those adjustments that would support the mission and values.

One of his key strategies was to initiate the most comprehensive restructuring process in the university's history and thereby to make the budget transparent. It was then that many on campus learned that some units were shouldering far more of the burden than others. After thoughtful discussions with the campus community, he drafted a restructuring report that disproportionately cut administrative units in favor of academic units. Units with the greatest potential were given budget increments, while others dealt with cuts as high as 50 percent. He also used this time to put forward 33 initiatives for positive change that provided the community with concrete ways to serve the institution's mission and vision.

Today, Syracuse is a greatly improved institution that is far, far more than its national championship men's basketball team. It has made dramatic gains in quality and reputation. More than 40 percent of new students come from the top 10 percent of their high school classes, and nearly 80 percent graduate in six years or less. The most recent capital campaign garnered almost $400 million, and sponsored research tops $60 million a year. The university was chosen as the site for a multimillion-dollar center for the study of indoor environmental quality, and several new research enterprises are showing great promise.

A comprehensive academic plan has challenged the university to strive for excellence in such areas as information management and technology, environmental quality, collaborative design, and citizenship and social transformation. It is matched by an equally ambitious space plan that, with a combination of new construction and renovations, will ready the campus for the twenty-first century and beyond.

Today Buzz Shaw is one of the most admired leaders in American higher education. Wherever this transformational leader has served, things have invariably improved.

## TIMOTHY R. THYREEN, WAYNESBURG COLLEGE

Few presidents have had more impact on their institutions than Timothy R. Thyreen. Thirteen years ago, Thyreen became president of a struggling institution. His tenure spans the most remarkable period in the 153-year history of the college. While he is not a revolutionary, virtually all know him as a risk taker, one who takes measured gambles. Thyreen has been a relentless, inexhaustible, passionate, intensely competitive force who has brought Waynesburg College regional and national recognition. He is widely respected and admired by individuals in every one of the college's constituencies, including his fellow college presidents in Pennsylvania and across the nation.

Waynesburg College has been transformed and refocused; it has recorded its highest enrollments, developed innovative curricular offerings, attracted superior faculty and staff, redeveloped and beautified its physical plant, and stabilized its financial resources. Its commitment to service learning as a core requirement has become a defining characteristic of the campus and is a national model. Perhaps the most visible evidence of the extraordinary transformation that has taken place under Thyreen's leadership is the campus itself. According to Carl Johnson, highly regarded master planner,

"Having participated in the authorship of scores of master plans for small colleges up to large mega system universities during 50 years of professional planning, I can honestly say I have never experienced a renaissance equal to that of Waynesburg College."

Particularly noteworthy during a secular age, President Thyreen made a visible commitment to renew the college's Christian higher education mission. This vision has attracted considerable foundation support. Dr. Corella A. Bonner, chair and cofounder of The Corella & Bertram F. Bonner Foundation in Princeton, New Jersey, stated that, "Waynesburg College offers the promise of what students, the college, and the community can do together once they realize and embrace their common commitment. Students' lives are transformed, the local community is revitalized, and the college issues a healthy challenge to society of what higher education is called to be."

Those who believe that presidents are as interchangeable as lightbulbs should visit Waynesburg College and talk to its faculty and staff. There may be some lightbulbs among American college presidents, but Timothy Thyreen obviously is not one of them.

## STEPHEN JOEL TRACHTENBERG, GEORGE WASHINGTON UNIVERSITY

When Stephen Trachtenberg became president of George Washington University, the word was that he would bring new life to the university, and that's exactly what happened. Trachtenberg's hand touched everything at GW: admissions, administrative and faculty appointments and evaluations, academic programs, governance, capital improvements, budgeting, fund-raising, administrative organization, and public relations. Today, GW's flag flies with the top universities in the country.

Fifteen years ago, GW had 6,000 applications for the freshman class; now it has 18,000. The university became more selective even while it expanded the size of its student body. SAT scores have gone up significantly; geographic, racial, and socioeconomic measures have been improved; and the endowment has climbed from $241 million to $578 million.

GW's Foggy Bottom campus was hemmed in by neighbors and couldn't grow. To accommodate more and better students, the university invested in replacing small buildings with larger ones and renovating others to get more space out of them. In 1999, GW bought Mount Vernon College, which was located in a suburban, almost bucolic, neighborhood of the District of Columbia, thus substantially expanding the capacity of residence halls, classrooms, sports facilities, and more at a stroke. GW also opened a new campus in Loudoun County, in the heart of the northern Virginia technology corridor.

The George Washington University is now recognized as a "hot" campus by prospective students and is widely acknowledged as an important player in the affairs of the Capitol Region. Many of its faculty have legitimate national reputations and are called upon by federal agencies for their expertise. Few would dispute that GW is the lengthened shadow of Stephen Joel Trachtenberg, a transformational president of the highest order.

## FINAL THOUGHTS

We have no cryptic, Delphic maxims to drop on the heads of readers of this final section. Yet a reasonable reading of the evidence we have introduced in chapters 4 through 6, plus the inspiring examples we have just provided of more than a dozen presidents who have transformed their campuses, should lay to rest the notion that an American college presidency must be a transactional, maintenance-oriented post that attracts and retains individuals who ultimately make little or no difference on their campuses. *Presidents are neither standardized lightbulbs nor pieces of Lego plastic that somehow can be inserted without visible pain or gain into any situation, with barely a notice of their service years later. In fact, a group of transformational, entrepreneurial presidents does exist today (our effective presidents), and these individuals are dynamic leaders, respectful of the roots of their institutions and the people with whom they work, but never fearful of leading and even anticipating necessary change.*

As the preceding profiles reveal, our transformational, entrepreneurial presidents are energetic, charismatic, exciting individuals who perceive opportunities where others see only gloom and disaster. They sense the transcendent possibilities of situations and, though committed to discussion and seeking consensus, are not afraid to disrupt the status quo. Some regard them as miracle makers. But they do not magically turn water into wine. Instead, they are individuals who generate synergy in their institutions and seem almost mysteriously to possess the ability to draw the best from their colleagues. Their energy and commitment are infectious; they inspire seemingly unattached outsiders to make exceedingly generous gifts in support of their visions.

To paraphrase Walter Lippmann (Peter, 1977, 298), our transformational, entrepreneurial presidents become the custodians of a renewed and extended set of ideals for their institutions. But they do so by preserving and enriching their institutions' traditions and ideals and by boldly confronting the real world. They do not shrink from change and are not repelled by intelligently calculated risks. Instead, they wisely assess their circumstances, consult with their colleagues, attract partners and supporters, and devise action plans that improve their campuses. Repeatedly, we have been told that the presidential tenures of our transformational, entrepreneurial presidents constitute the most exhilarating times these campuses have ever experienced.

Of course, not all transformational, entrepreneurial presidencies receive such high marks, and occasionally the equivalent of an institutional plane crash occurs. One should not conclude that every notion labeled *entrepreneurial* is praiseworthy or genuine. Nor should one deduce that transformational presidencies always succeed. Even so, transactional, representative presidents are unlikely to inspire the praise and superlatives directed to our transformational, entrepreneurial presidents. All too often, transactional presidents are deaf to the sound of opportunity, and hence their campuses slowly stagnate and fall short of potential. Theirs may be a comfortable presidency, but they underperform in their positions and leave student and faculty potential to rot on the institutional table.

Do our transformational, entrepreneurial presidents equal the titans of the past? It depends how one measures such things (Dennison, 2001). If, however, one's standard is improved student and faculty welfare, increased opportunities for students to learn, and an enhanced ability for faculty to teach and research, then these inspiring individuals are indeed titans, for they have dramatically changed and improved the worlds around them. Not a shabby legacy, that.

> It is not the critic that counts, nor the man who points out how the strong man stumbled or where the doer of deeds could have done them better. The credit belongs to the man in the arena; whose face is marred by dust and sweat and blood; who strives valiantly; who errs and comes up short again and again; who knows the great enthusiasm, the great devotion, and spends himself in worthy cause; who at the best, knows in the end the triumph of high achievement, and who at the worst, if he fails while daring greatly, knows his place shall never be with those cold and timid souls who know neither victory nor defeat.
>
> Theodore Roosevelt, President of the United States, 1901–1909

# Appendix A: Letter
# Seeking Nominations

16 January 2002

Dear Academic Colleague:

Almost 15 years ago, James L. Fisher, Martha W. Tack, and Karen J. Wheeler published *The Effective College President*, the first statistically rigorous and replicable empirical study of what makes some college presidents more effective and successful than others. Funded by the Exxon Foundation, their work firmly established that exceptionally effective college presidents are different from all other presidents in terms of how they see their jobs, do their work, and relate to others.

Now, funded by the Kauffman Foundation, we are testing and extending the Fisher/Tack/Wheeler study. Our special focus is on entrepreneurial presidents, but we also are giving additional attention to women and minority presidents, whose numbers have swelled considerably in recent years. Are they different from other presidents?

However, in order for us to proceed, we need your help! *We would like you to nominate up to six sitting college presidents as "especially effective, especially successful" in their jobs.* Please use your own definition of effectiveness.

Please use this sheet and the attached, postage paid envelope to send us up to six of your nominations. Do not hesitate to contact us at jkoch@ odu.edu should you have any questions or suggestions.

Sincerely,

James V. Koch                          James L. Fisher

Board of Visitors Professor            President Emeritus,
of Economics                           Towson University,
and President Emeritus,                 and President Emeritus,
Old Dominion University                 Council for the Advancement
                                        and Support of Education

## MY "MOST EFFECTIVE PRESIDENT" NOMINEES ARE:

_____     _____     _____

_____     _____     _____

# Appendix B: Effective Leadership Inventory

*Directions:* This questionnaire is designed to identify the characteristics of an effective college president (chancellor) and focuses on three areas: styles/attitudes, professional information, and personal data. Please provide the information in the format requested

## PART I: PERSONAL ATTITUDES AND LEADERSHIP STYLE

Please react to the following statements about your own characteristics as a leader by checking the appropriate responses. Your responses should represent your perceptions of yourself as a leader.

SA =Strongly Agree     A= Agree     UD = Undecided
D= Disagree     SD= Strongly Disagree

| As a college president, I: | SA | A | UD | D | SD |
|---|---|---|---|---|---|
| 1. Am sometimes viewed as hard-nosed. | [ ] | [ ] | [ ] | [ ] | [ ] |
| 2. Believe that respect from those I lead is crucial. | [ ] | [ ] | [ ] | [ ] | [ ] |
| 3. Believe that an effective leader takes risks. | [ ] | [ ] | [ ] | [ ] | [ ] |
| 4. Place a high value on consensus. | [ ] | [ ] | [ ] | [ ] | [ ] |
| 5. Believe in organizational structure. | [ ] | [ ] | [ ] | [ ] | [ ] |
| 6. Believe that the leader should be perceived as self-confident. | [ ] | [ ] | [ ] | [ ] | [ ] |
| 7. Believe in close collegial relationships with faculty. | [ ] | [ ] | [ ] | [ ] | [ ] |
| 8. Believe that a leader serves the people. | [ ] | [ ] | [ ] | [ ] | [ ] |

|     |                                                                 | SA  | A   | UD  | D   | SD  |
|-----|-----------------------------------------------------------------|-----|-----|-----|-----|-----|
| 9.  | Believe in merit pay.                                           | [ ] | [ ] | [ ] | [ ] | [ ] |
| 10. | Am sometimes viewed as assertive.                               | [ ] | [ ] | [ ] | [ ] | [ ] |
| 11. | Frequently violate the status quo.                              | [ ] | [ ] | [ ] | [ ] | [ ] |
| 12. | Delegate responsibility and authority to subordinates.          | [ ] | [ ] | [ ] | [ ] | [ ] |
| 13. | Believe in the value of one-on-one meetings.                    | [ ] | [ ] | [ ] | [ ] | [ ] |
| 14. | Believe the economy's failed dot.com firms provide a cautionary lesson for higher education. | [ ] | [ ] | [ ] | [ ] | [ ] |
| 15. | Always use social and athletic functions as opportunities to promote my institution. | [ ] | [ ] | [ ] | [ ] | [ ] |
| 16. | Accept losses gracefully.                                       | [ ] | [ ] | [ ] | [ ] | [ ] |
| 17. | Maintain a measure of mystique.                                 | [ ] | [ ] | [ ] | [ ] | [ ] |
| 18. | Am more likely than most presidents to consider alternative methods of delivering higher education. | [ ] | [ ] | [ ] | [ ] | [ ] |
| 19. | Choose another CEO as a confidant.                              | [ ] | [ ] | [ ] | [ ] | [ ] |
| 20. | Am highly involved in the community.                            | [ ] | [ ] | [ ] | [ ] | [ ] |
| 21. | Always appear energetic.                                        | [ ] | [ ] | [ ] | [ ] | [ ] |
| 22. | Am often viewed as a loner.                                     | [ ] | [ ] | [ ] | [ ] | [ ] |
| 23. | Count committee meetings as mistakes                            | [ ] | [ ] | [ ] | [ ] | [ ] |
| 24. | Would rather be viewed as a strong leader than as a good colleague. | [ ] | [ ] | [ ] | [ ] | [ ] |
| 25. | Tend to work long hours.                                        | [ ] | [ ] | [ ] | [ ] | [ ] |
| 26. | Often like people who are different.                            | [ ] | [ ] | [ ] | [ ] | [ ] |
| 27. | Only occasionally speak spontaneously.                          | [ ] | [ ] | [ ] | [ ] | [ ] |
| 28. | Participate actively in national higher education organizations. | [ ] | [ ] | [ ] | [ ] | [ ] |
| 29. | Dress well.                                                     | [ ] | [ ] | [ ] | [ ] | [ ] |
| 30. | Care deeply about the welfare of the individual.                | [ ] | [ ] | [ ] | [ ] | [ ] |
| 31. | Put my institution before myself.                               | [ ] | [ ] | [ ] | [ ] | [ ] |
| 32. | Encourage creative individuals even even though we may disagree. | [ ] | [ ] | [ ] | [ ] | [ ] |
| 33. | Appear to make decisions easily.                                | [ ] | [ ] | [ ] | [ ] | [ ] |
| 34. | Appear confident even when in doubt                             | [ ] | [ ] | [ ] | [ ] | [ ] |
| 35. | Have made decisions that could have resulted in my losing my job if the results had turned out badly | [ ] | [ ] | [ ] | [ ] | [ ] |
| 36. | Am often seen as somewhat aloof.                                | [ ] | [ ] | [ ] | [ ] | [ ] |
| 37. | Enjoy stirring things up.                                       | [ ] | [ ] | [ ] | [ ] | [ ] |
| 38. | Am rarely viewed as flamboyant.                                 | [ ] | [ ] | [ ] | [ ] | [ ] |
| 39. | Am feared by some.                                              | [ ] | [ ] | [ ] | [ ] | [ ] |
| 40. | Smile a lot.                                                    | [ ] | [ ] | [ ] | [ ] | [ ] |
| 41. | Believe fund-raising and development tasks are my highest priority. | [ ] | [ ] | [ ] | [ ] | [ ] |
| 42. | Would consider moving to a better position.                     | [ ] | [ ] | [ ] | [ ] | [ ] |

|     |                                                                          | SA  | A   | UD  | D   | SD  |
|-----|--------------------------------------------------------------------------|-----|-----|-----|-----|-----|
| 43. | Am viewed as politically adept.                                          | [ ] | [ ] | [ ] | [ ] | [ ] |
| 44. | Am viewed by faculty as a strongly academic person.                      | [ ] | [ ] | [ ] | [ ] | [ ] |
| 45. | View the faculty senate as a substantially useless appendage.            | [ ] | [ ] | [ ] | [ ] | [ ] |
| 46. | Have the strong support of my governing board.                           | [ ] | [ ] | [ ] | [ ] | [ ] |
| 47. | Have successfully concluded many partnerships involving business and government with my institution. | [ ] | [ ] | [ ] | [ ] | [ ] |
| 48. | Make many mistakes.                                                      | [ ] | [ ] | [ ] | [ ] | [ ] |
| 49. | Am burdened by a governing board that attempts to micromanage the institution. | [ ] | [ ] | [ ] | [ ] | [ ] |
| 50. | Am solely responsible for teaching a course at least once every two years. | [ ] | [ ] | [ ] | [ ] | [ ] |
| 51. | Generate many innovative ideas.                                         | [ ] | [ ] | [ ] | [ ] | [ ] |
| 52. | Believe the President is the final authority under the governing board on all matters affecting the institution. | [ ] | [ ] | [ ] | [ ] | [ ] |
| 53. | Believe faculty should make academic decisions.                         | [ ] | [ ] | [ ] | [ ] | [ ] |
| 54. | Am warm and affable.                                                    | [ ] | [ ] | [ ] | [ ] | [ ] |
| 55. | Believe intercollegiate athletics are in need of reform.                | [ ] | [ ] | [ ] | [ ] | [ ] |
| 56. | Spend a great deal of time dealing with the media and the press.        | [ ] | [ ] | [ ] | [ ] | [ ] |
| 57. | Frequently walk my campus and am seen by students and faculty.          | [ ] | [ ] | [ ] | [ ] | [ ] |
| 58. | Am viewed by minorities and women as highly supportive of them.         | [ ] | [ ] | [ ] | [ ] | [ ] |
| 59. | Am an internationalist in outlook.                                      | [ ] | [ ] | [ ] | [ ] | [ ] |
| 60. | Believe the campus involvement of my spouse or significant other is important. | [ ] | [ ] | [ ] | [ ] | [ ] |
| 61. | Believe all institutions need changing.                                 | [ ] | [ ] | [ ] | [ ] | [ ] |
| 62. | Respect the chain of command.                                           | [ ] | [ ] | [ ] | [ ] | [ ] |
| 63. | Believe in a flat organization.                                         | [ ] | [ ] | [ ] | [ ] | [ ] |
| 64. | Believe 8–10 years in office is long enough.                            | [ ] | [ ] | [ ] | [ ] | [ ] |
| 65. | Believe in frequent faculty meetings.                                   | [ ] | [ ] | [ ] | [ ] | [ ] |
| 66. | Believe in strategic planning.                                          | [ ] | [ ] | [ ] | [ ] | [ ] |
| 67. | Do not shy away from controversy.                                       | [ ] | [ ] | [ ] | [ ] | [ ] |
| 68. | Believe my primary role is to manage.                                   | [ ] | [ ] | [ ] | [ ] | [ ] |
| 69. | Am viewed as a risk taker.                                              | [ ] | [ ] | [ ] | [ ] | [ ] |
| 70. | Believe my primary role is to inspire.                                  | [ ] | [ ] | [ ] | [ ] | [ ] |
| 71. | Think administrators who report to me should agree with me, change my mind, or resign. | [ ] | [ ] | [ ] | [ ] | [ ] |

# PART II: PROFESSIONAL DATA

## Degrees Earned

*I hold a Doctoral degree :*          No   [ ]                    Yes   [ ]

*If yes, type of degree:*        Ph.D.   [ ]              JD   [ ]
          One or more honorary degrees   [ ]        Ed.D.   [ ]
                              MD   [ ]           Other   [ ]

*Institution Granting Degree:* _____

*Type of Institution:*          Public   [ ]        Private   [ ]

*Major:* _____

*I hold a Master's degree:*
No   [ ]              Yes   [ ]

*If yes, type of degree:*          MA, MS   [ ]          MBA   [ ]
                            M.Ed.   [ ]          MFA   [ ]          Other   [ ]

*Institution Granting Degree:* _____

*Type of Institution:*          Public   [ ]        Private   [ ]

*Major:* _____

*I hold a Baccalaureate degree:*    No   [ ]                    Yes   [ ]

*If yes, type of degree:*          BS   [ ]          BFA   [ ]
                            BA   [ ]          Other   [ ]

*Institution Granting Degree:* _____

*Type of Institution:*          Public   [ ]        Private   [ ]

*Coursework:* I have taken *two or more* courses in the following academic areas:
                    Economics   [ ]                         Accounting   [ ]
                    Statistics   [ ]                  Computer Science   [ ]

*Use of Technology:*

I use the Internet frequently          [ ]        I require the most important          [ ]
I use a computer frequently          [ ]        individuals who report to me
I carry a cell phone with me          [ ]        to carry a cell phone or
when I'm away from campus                    pager so I can reach them

# Previous Experience

*Positions Held in Higher Education.* Beginning with the first position, indicate the offices you have held using the codes listed below. When designating associate or assistant positions, codes should be combined, e.g., JE = assistant dean. If you changed institutions, but kept the same title, please make separate entries for each position occupied. Additionally, please refer to the institutional codes when identifying the type of institution at which you were employed.

|  | *Position Codes* | | *Institutional Codes* |
|---|---|---|---|
| A = Full-time faculty member | F = Assistant to the | | 1 = 4-year, public |
| B = Department chairperson | G = Vice President | | 2 = 4-year, private |
| C = Coordinator | H = President | | 3 = 2-year, public |
| D = Director | I = Associate | | 4 = 2-year, private |
| E = Dean | J = Assistant | | |
|  | K = Other | | |

| *Position Chronology* | *Position Code* | *Academic Dept. or Admin. Area* | *Years in Position* | *Institution Type* |
|---|---|---|---|---|
| E.g., | A | Economics | 7 | 1 |
| 1 | | | | |
| 2 | | | | |
| 3 | | | | |
| 4 | | | | |
| 5 | | | | |
| 6 | | | | |
| 7 | | | | |
| 8 | | | | |
| 9 | | | | |
| 10 | | | | |
| 11 | | | | |
| 12 | | | | |

Total Years in Higher
Education Administration: _____

Total Years of Experience Outside
of Higher Education: _____

Total Years in
Presidential Position: _____

Age upon Assumption of
First Presidency: _____

## Current Position

Years in Current Presidency: _____

*Type of Institution:*       Public      [ ]        Private      [ ]
                             Two-Year  [ ]        Four-Year  [ ]

*Student Population* (headcount)        *Published Salary:*      _____
*of my campus:*              _____

## Scholarly Activity

Number of Books Published: _____

Approximate Number of Articles in Refereed Journals:   _____

Approximate Number of Professional Organization Memberships:  _____

Two Professional Organizations in Which You Participate Frequently:

Organization No. 1:   _____

Office(s) Held:   _____

Organization No. 2:   _____

Office(s) Held:   _____

## Positions Outside of Higher Education:

Immediately prior to assuming my first presidency,      [ ]
I held a position outside of higher education

Prior to becoming a college president, I was           [ ]
the CEO or equivalent of a business firm,
foundation, or governmental agency

The total number of years I have spent as a full-time employee outside
of higher education is: _____

# PART III: PERSONAL INFORMATION

*Age:*_____

| | | | |
|---|---|---|---|
| *Sex:* | Male [ ] | Female [ ] | |

*Race:*
| | | | |
|---|---|---|---|
| Native American [ ] | Hispanic/Latino [ ] |
| Asian American [ ] | Caucasian [ ] |
| African American [ ] | Other [ ] |

*Religion:*
| | |
|---|---|
| Eastern Orthodox [ ] | Baptist [ ] |
| Jewish [ ] | Episcopal [ ] |
| Muslim [ ] | Methodist [ ] |
| Roman Catholic [ ] | Presbyterian [ ] |
| Lutheran [ ] | Other Protestant [ ] |
| Other [ ] | |

*Marital Status:*
| | | *Number of Marriages:* | |
|---|---|---|---|
| Never Married [ ] | | 0 [ ] |
| Divorced [ ] | | 1 [ ] |
| Widowed [ ] | | 2 [ ] |
| Now Married [ ] | | 3 [ ] |
| | | 4+ [ ] |

*My spouse or significant other is:*

Employed full-time [ ]    Employed part-time [ ]

Contributes substantial uncompensated time to my institution [ ]

Does not attend many major institutional activities such [ ]
as graduations, athletic contests and social events

Is compensated by the institution for his/her contributions [ ]

*Number of Children:*
| | *Ages of Children:* | |
|---|---|---|
| 0 [ ] | _____ |
| 1 [ ] | _____ |
| 2 [ ] | _____ |
| 3 [ ] | _____ |
| 4 [ ] | _____ |
| 5+ [ ] | _____ |

*State or Foreign Country of Birth:* _____

*State of Current Residence:* _____

*Political Affiliation:*
| | | |
|---|---|---|
| Independent [ ] | Democrat [ ] |
| Republican [ ] | Other [ ] |

*Father's Education:*
| | |
|---|---|
| Less Than High School [ ] | Post-Baccalaureate Courses [ ] |
| Some High School [ ] | Master's Degree [ ] |
| High School Diploma [ ] | Doctoral Degree [ ] |
| College Courses [ ] | Post-Doctoral Work [ ] |
| Baccalaureate Degree [ ] | |

*Mother's Education:*
| | |
|---|---|
| Less Than High School [ ] | Post-Baccalaureate Courses [ ] |
| Some High School [ ] | Master's Degree [ ] |
| High School Diploma [ ] | Doctoral Degree [ ] |
| College Courses [ ] | Post-Doctoral Work [ ] |
| Baccalaureate Degree [ ] | |

*Number of Siblings:*
| | |
|---|---|
| Younger Brothers _____ | Older Brothers _____ |
| Younger Sisters _____ | Older Sisters _____ |

## Please return this instrument in the attached envelope to:

James V. Koch                    or          James V. Koch
Board of Visitors Professor                  240 Keith Avenue
of Economics and                             Missoula, MT 59801–4308
President Emeritus
Department of Economics
Old Dominion University
Norfolk, VA 23529

If you have questions, e-mail James V. Koch at Jkoch@odu.edu.

# Appendix C: Letter to Nominated Presidents

6 March 2002

Dear Academic Colleague:

*We need your help!* Almost 15 years ago, James L. Fisher, Martha W. Tack, and Karen J. Wheeler published *The Effective College President*, the first statistically rigorous and replicable empirical study of what makes some college presidents more effective and successful than others. Funded by the Exxon Foundation, their work firmly established that exceptionally effective college presidents are different from all other presidents in terms of how they see their jobs, do their work, and relate to others.

Now, funded by the Kauffman Foundation, we are testing and extending the Fisher/Tack/Wheeler study. Our special focus is on entrepreneurial presidents, but we also are giving additional attention to women and minority presidents, whose numbers have swelled considerably in recent years. Are they different from other presidents?

However, in order for us to proceed, we need your help! *You have been nominated as an especially effective and successful president. Now, we would like you to complete the attached survey form so we can learn more about the attitudes and activities of especially effective presidents such as you.*

Please use the attached, postage paid envelope to send us your survey. Do not hesitate to contact us at jkoch@odu.edu should you have any questions or suggestions.

Sincerely,

James V. Koch                          James L. Fisher

Board of Visitors Professor            President Emeritus,
of Economics                           Towson University,
and President Emeritus,                 and President Emeritus,
Old Dominion University                 Council for the Advancement
                                       and Support of Education


## MY "MOST EFFECTIVE PRESIDENT" NOMINEES ARE:

_____        _____        _____

_____        _____        _____

# Appendix D: Letter to Unnominated Presidents

6 March 2002

Dear Academic Colleague:

*We need your help!* Almost 15 years ago, James L. Fisher, Martha W. Tack, and Karen J. Wheeler published *The Effective College President*, the first statistically rigorous and replicable empirical study of what makes some college presidents more effective and successful than others. Funded by the Exxon Foundation, their work firmly established that exceptionally effective college presidents are different from all other presidents in terms of how they see their jobs, do their work, and relate to others.

Now, funded by the Kauffman Foundation, we are testing and extending the Fisher/Tack/Wheeler study. Our special focus is on entrepreneurial presidents, but we also are giving additional attention to women and minority presidents, whose numbers have swelled considerably in recent years. Are they different from other presidents?

However, in order for us to proceed, we need your help! *We would like you to complete the attached survey form so we can learn more about the attitudes and activities of sitting presidents such as you.*

Please use the attached, postage paid envelope to send us your survey. Do not hesitate to contact us at jkoch@odu.edu should you have any questions or suggestions.

Sincerely,

James V. Koch                                   James L. Fisher

Board of Visitors Professor            President Emeritus,
of Economics                                   Towson University,
and President Emeritus,                  and President Emeritus,
Old Dominion University                Council for the Advancement
                                                         and Support of Education


## MY "MOST EFFECTIVE PRESIDENT" NOMINEES ARE:

_____        _____        _____

_____        _____        _____

# Appendix E: Data Sources

Most of the data utilized in the study were obtained from the survey instrument. The sources of the other data used were as follows:

| | |
|---|---|
| Carnegie Institutional Classification, 2000 | Carnegie Foundation for the Advancement of Teaching. *The Carnegie Classification of Institutions of Higher Education.* Washington, D.C.: Carnegie Commission, 2000. |
| Annual Budget, 2001 | Council for Aid to Education. *2001 Voluntary Support of Education.* New York: CAE, 2002. |
| Tuition and Fees, 2001 | |
| Freshmen Applications Accepted (%, 2001) | *U.S. News and World Report. America's Best Colleges,* 2003 Edition. Washington, D.C.: U.S. News and World Report, 2002. |
| SAT Verbal Midrange, 2001 | *U.S. News and World Report, 2002* |
| ACT Midrange, 2001 | *U.S. News and World Report, 2002* |
| Freshmen with GPA ≥ 3.00 (%, 2001) | *U.S. News and World Report, 2002* |
| Freshmen in Top 10% of HS Class, 2001 | *U.S. News and World Report, 2002* |
| Freshmen Retention (%, 2001) | *U.S. News and World Report, 2002* |
| Freshmen Out of State (%, 2001) | *U.S. News and World Report, 2002* |
| Freshmen Minorities (%, 2001) | *U.S. News and World Report, 2002* |
| Freshmen ≥ 25 Years (%, 2001) | *U.S. News and World Report, 2002* |

| | |
|---|---|
| Undergraduate Women (%, 2001) | *U.S. News and World Report, 2002* |
| Classes ≤ 20 (%, 2001) | *U.S. News and World Report, 2002* |
| Student/Faculty Ratio, 2001 | *U.S. News and World Report, 2002* |
| Full-Time Faculty (%, 2001) | *U.S. News and World Report, 2002* |
| Six-Year Graduation Rate | *U.S. News and World Report, 2002* |
| *U.S. News* Peer Rating, 2001 | *U.S. News and World Report, 2002* |
| Endowment, 2001 | Council for Aid to Education (CAE), 2002 |
| Endowment, 1995 | CAE, 1996 |
| Gifts Received, 2001 | CAE, 2002 |
| Gifts Received, 1995 | CAE, 1996 |
| Alumni Making Gifts (%, 2001) | CAE, 2002 |
| Alumni Making Gifts (%, 1995) | CAE, 1996 |
| Gifts Coming from Top 12 Donors (%, 2001) | CAE, 2002 |
| Gifts Coming from Top 12 Donors (%, 1995) | CAE, 1996 |

# Notes

## CHAPTER 1: THE NOTION OF THE ENTREPRENEURIAL LEADER

1. In the remainder of the book, we will use the terms *college president*, *university president*, and *college and university president* interchangeably and as synonyms for each other.

2. The eminent twentieth-century economist Frank Knight distinguished between "risk" and "uncertainty." A risky situation is one in which the probability distribution of outcomes is known, even though what actually will happen is unknown. Thus, if one flips a fair coin, there is a probability of .5 that either a head or a tail will appear. One doesn't know which event will occur if one flips the coin, but the probability distribution is known a priori. "Uncertainty," on the other hand, is a situation in which the probability distribution of outcomes is unknown; for instance, it is unknown what is the precise probability of a terrorist attack on the San Francisco Bay Bridge. Clearly, there are degrees of uncertainty. In some situations, one may not even know the range of possible outcomes. In other situations, one may know the possible outcomes, but not their probabilities of occurrence. In a "pure" uncertain situation, one does not have the foggiest idea about what events could occur. This is only rarely true in higher education. Frank H. Knight, *Risk, Uncertainty and Profit* (Boston: Houghton-Mifflin, 1921).

## CHAPTER 2: A REVIEW OF RELEVANT WORK

1. Fisher, Tack, and Wheeler (1984) catalogued 33 distinct characteristics of successful college presidents, including adjectives such as "courageous," "charismatic," and the like. This naturally leads to the question, "Well, what characteristics and attitudes are most important to presidential success?" That was the focus of the Fisher, Tack, and Wheeler study, as well as the work reported in this book.

2. Bok's position, however, is not as absolute as it at first seems. He now says, "Yet profit seeking has undoubtedly helped in some instances to improve academic work and to enhance higher education's value to society" (Bok, 2003a, B7).

3. Less poetically, Collins and Porras (1996) speak repeatedly of "big hairy audacious goals."

## CHAPTER 3: MATTERS OF PROCESS

1. This is a version of the classic "free rider" problem that afflicts many charitable endeavors and social services. What incentive does an individual have to contribute resources to the Red Cross if he/she knows that the Red Cross will support him/her even if no contribution is made? The tendency, therefore, is for some (perhaps many) individuals not to support the Red Cross financially. Or, in a different situation, citizens may not pick up trash in a public park because even if they do not, someone else (perhaps the government) ultimately will. So also it is with surveys, even ones that are perceived to be important. "Let the other guy fill it out and then I'll read the results" appears to be an unspoken, but strong tendency for many time-pressured presidents. It might well be, therefore, that presidents of larger, more complex institutions and highly compensated presidents have the tendency to reply to surveys less often.

## CHAPTER 4: THE 713 PRESIDENTS IN OUR SAMPLE

1. An anonymous reviewer suggested that while the ACE believes its sample generates a balanced picture of American college presidents, the ACE does not purport that its sample and data are "fully representational" of the universe of college presidents. By extension, the same might be said about our survey and data.

2. Equal variances were assumed when the null hypothesis that the variances of the two variables were equal was accepted at the .10 level of statistical significance or better.

3. Dennison (2001) has suggested that the alleged absence of "presidential giants" in modern times may be due at least partially to the diminishing tenures of presidents. Perhaps presidents do not stay long enough to become giants!

4. We are reminded of the case of the president of a flagship public university who, just days prior to his state's gubernatorial election, appeared on television in advertisements for a candidate who subsequently was defeated. This caused a major controversy and, according to news accounts, caused the newly elected governor to hang up on the president abruptly during their first telephone conversation.

5. Cotton (2003) also reported that 23 percent of the spouses of a sample of independent college presidents were compensated for their contributions. He reported that one spouse of a sitting president is compensated $68,000 per year.

6. Certain religious institutions legally may require their president to be unmarried.

7. Note that FTW utilized a "reversed" Likert scale such that strong agreement was assigned a value of 1 and strong disagreement a value of 5. Our scale assigns a higher number to stronger agreement and a lower number to stronger disagreement. Thus, the reader should tread carefully as she compares FTW's statistical results with ours.

## CHAPTER 5: GENDER, RACE, AND THE AMERICAN COLLEGE PRESIDENCY

1. By contrast, the percent of women who hold *one of the five highest jobs* at a Fortune 500 company was only 7.9 percent (Jones 2003).

2. We readily note that the variations inside the group of minority presidents in certain cases may be as large as, or even exceed, those between minority presidents as a group and all other presidents as a group. That is, in some circumstances, the differences, say, between Asian American presidents and African American presidents may exceed those between all minority presidents as a group and all Caucasian presidents as a group. However, the paucity of presidents in each ethnic category forced us to aggregate them into a single group for purposes of statistical analysis.

3. Separate from this is the question whether discrimination is responsible for women presidents exhibiting these less-favorable demographic characteristics in the first place.

4. Once again, we caution the reader that few, if any, two-year colleges are included in the subsample that generated these conclusions. These generalizations apply almost exclusively to four-year institutions, and only 52 observations exist for women presidents for the graduation rate variable.

5. Note that there is substantial overlap between men presidents and Caucasian presidents. Approximately four-fifths of all Caucasian presidents are men.

## CHAPTER 6: THE ENTREPRENEURIAL PRESIDENT

1. We again point out that there is substantial overlap between men and Caucasian presidents. Approximately four-fifths of all Caucasian presidents are men.

2. Boards that discourage presidential teaching and research, however, may face a dilemma when that individual's presidential tenure ends—for whatever reason. What should they do with the former president? If the president no longer is viable as a teacher/scholar, then literally he may have nothing to do and may become an embarrassing and useless appendage on and around the campus, and possibly a troublemaker to boot. They may then have to "buy" a position for him, either on- or off-campus, because he is no longer suited for a legitimate faculty position.

3. We issue two caveats here. First, paraphrasing Frederick the Great, experience is valuable only if one divines the right lessons from it. Some leaders extract erroneous lessons from history. Second, there are diminishing returns to additional experience. Thus, after a president has spent 7 to 10 years in her presidency, each additional year is much less valuable.

# References

American Council on Education. 2002. *The American College President, 2002 Edition*. Washington, D.C.: American Council on Education.

Association of Governing Boards of Universities and Colleges. 1996. *Renewing the Academic Presidency: Stronger Leadership for Tougher Times*. Washington, D.C.: Association of Governing Boards of Universities and Colleges.

Atkinson, Brooks, ed. 1940. *The Complete Essays and Other Writings of Ralph Waldo Emerson*. New York: Modern Library.

Axelrod, Paul. 2003. *Values in Conflict: The University, the Marketplace, and the Trials of Liberal Education*. Montreal: McGill-Queen's University Press.

Balderston, Frederick E. 1995. *Managing Today's University*. 2d ed. San Francisco: Jossey-Bass.

Bass, Bernard M. 1990. *Bass and Stodgill's Handbook of Leadership: Theory, Research, and Managerial Applications*. 3rd ed. New York: Free Press.

Bénezét, Louis T., Joseph Katz, and Frances W. Magnusson. 1981. *Style and Substance: Leadership and the College Presidency*. Washington, D.C.: American Council on Education.

Bennis, Warren G., and Burt Nanus. 1985. *Leaders: The Strategies for Taking Charge*. New York: Harper and Row.

Berendzen, Richard. 1986. *Is My Armor on Straight? A Year in the Life of a University President*. Bethesda, Md.: Adler and Adler.

Berle, Adolf A., and Gardiner C. Means. 1932. *The Modern Corporation and Private Property*. New York: Commerce Clearing House.

Bielec, John. 2002. "When Universities Act Like Businesses." *University Business* 5 (November): 9.

Birnbaum, Robert. 1988. *How Colleges Work: The Cybernetics of Academic Organization and Leadership*. San Francisco: Jossey-Bass.

———. 1992. *How Academic Leadership Works: Understanding Success and Failure in the College Presidency*. San Francisco: Jossey-Bass.

———. 2000. *Management Fads in Higher Education*. San Francisco: Jossey-Bass.

Bok, Derek. 2003a. "Academic Values and the Lure of Profit." *Chronicle of Higher Education* 49 (4 April 2003): B7–9.

———. 2003b. *Universities in the Marketplace: The Commercialization of Higher Education*. Princeton, N.J.: Princeton University Press.

Bolman, F. 1965. *How College Presidents Are Chosen*. Washington, D.C.: American Council on Education.

Boone, Louis E. 1992. *Quotable Business*. New York: Random House.

Botstein, Leon. 1985. "Leadership: Golden Rules of Practice." In *Opportunity in Adversity: How Colleges Can Succeed in Hard Times*, edited by Janice S. Green et al., pp. 105–25. San Francisco: Jossey-Bass.

Budig, Gene. 2002. *A Game of Uncommon Skill: Leading the Modern College and University*. Westport, Conn.: Oryx/ACE.

Burke, Edmund. 1909. *Reflections on the Revolution in France, 1790*. Harvard Classics, vol. 24, part 3. New York: P.F. Collier and Company.

Burns, John M. 1978. *Leadership*. New York: Harper and Row.

———. 2003. *Transforming Leadership: A New Pursuit of Happiness*. Berkeley, Calif.: Atlantic Monthly Press.

Cameron, Kim S., and David A. Whetten, eds. 1983. *Organizational Effectiveness: A Comparison of Multiple Models*. New York: Academic Press.

Carnegie Council on Policy Studies in Higher Education. 1980. *Three Thousand Futures: The Next Twenty Years for Higher Education*. San Francisco: Jossey-Bass.

Carnegie Foundation for the Advancement of Teaching. 2000. *The Carnegie Classification of Institutions of Higher Education*. Washington, D.C.: Carnegie Commission.

Carter, Stephen. 1992. *Reflections of an Affirmative Action Baby*. New York: Basic Books.

Chliwniak, Luba. 1997. *Higher Education Leadership: Analyzing the Gender Gap*. Washington, D.C.: George Washington University/ASHE/ERIC, 1997.

Christ, Carl. 1993. "Assessing Econometric Results." *Federal Reserve Bank of St. Louis Review* 75, no. 2: 71–94.

*Chronicle of Higher Education*. 2003. "Potent Partnerships." *Chronicle of Higher Education* 49 (10 January): A24.

Cohen, Michael D., and James G. March. 1986. *Leadership and Ambiguity: The American College President*. Rev. ed. Boston: Harvard Business School Press.

Collins, James C., and Jerry I. Porras. 1996. *Built to Last: Successful Habits of Visionary Companies*. New York: Harper Business.

Cotton, Raymond D. 2003. "Paying the President's Spouse." *Chronicle of Higher Education* 44 (23 May 2003): C5.

Council for Aid to Education. 1996. *Voluntary Support of Education 1995*. New York: Council for Aid to Education.

Council for the Advancement and Support of Education. 2002. *2001 Voluntary Support of Education*. New York: Council for Aid to Education.

Crowley, Joseph N. 1994. *No Equal in the World: An Interpretation of the Academic Presidency*. Reno: University of Nevada.

Dahl, R.A. 1957. "The Concepts of Power." *Behavioral Science* 2:201–15.

Dennison, George M. 2001. "Small Men on Campus: Modern University Presidents." *Innovative Higher Education* 25 (Summer): 269–84.

*Encarta World English Dictionary.* 1999. New York: St. Martin's Press.

Ferrari, Michael R. 1970. "Profiles of American college presidents." Unpublished doctoral dissertation, Division of Research, Graduate School of Business Administration, Michigan State University, East Lansing, Mich.

Fisher, James L. 1984. *Power of the Presidency*. San Francisco: Jossey-Bass.

Fisher, James L., and James V. Koch. 1996. *Presidential Leadership: Making a Difference*. Phoenix, Ariz.: American Council on Education/Oryx.

Fisher, James L., and Martha W. Tack. 1988. *Leaders on Leadership: The College Presidency*. San Francisco: Jossey-Bass.

Fisher, James L., Martha W. Tack, and Karen J. Wheeler. 1988. *The Effective College President*. New York: American Council on Education/MacMillan.

French, J.R.P., and B.H. Raven. 1959. "The Bases of Social Power." In *Studies in Social Power*, edited by D. Cartwright. Ann Arbor, Mich.: University of Michigan, Institute for Social Research.

Friedman, Milton, and Anna J. Schwartz. 1991. "Alternative Approaches to Analyzing Economic Data." *American Economic Review* 81 (March): 39–49.

Gaona, Elena. 2003. "For 25 Years, A Firm Hand on the Helm: Harvey Puts His Stamp on HU with Bricks, Bravado." *The Newport News, Virginia Daily Press* (27 April 2003). http://www.pqasb.pqarchiver.com/dailypress/doc/3296221421.html.

Gardner, John W. 1986. *The Heart of the Matter: Leader-Constituent Interaction*. Leadership Papers/3. Washington, D.C.: Independent Sector.

Gardner, R.G., and M.D. Brown. 1973. *Personal Characteristics of Community College Presidents*. ERIC Document Reproduction Service No. ED 104456.

Garten, Jeffrey. 2003. "Listen Up Execs: Playing It Safe Won't Cut It." *Business Week*, 3 March, 28.

Gerstner, Louis V. 2002. *Who Says Elephants Can't Dance? Inside IBM's Turnaround*. New York: Harper Collins.

Getz, Malcolm, John J. Siegfried, and Kathryn H. Anderson. 1997. "Adoptions of Innovations in Higher Education." *Quarterly Review of Economics and Finance* 37 (Fall): 605–31.

Gilley, J. Wade, K.A. Fulmer, and S.J. Reithlingshoefer. 1986. *Searching for Academic Excellence: Twenty Colleges and Universities on the Move and Their Leaders*. New York: American Council on Education/MacMillan.

Greenberg, Daniel S. 1998. "The Shrinking College President: Small Men on Campus." *The New Republic* (1 June): 18–21.

Hamel, Gary, and Peter Skarzynski. 2002. "Innovation: The New Route to New Wealth." In *On Creativity, Innovation and Renewal*, edited by Francis Hesselbein and Rob Johnston. San Francisco: Jossey-Bass.

Harris Interactive. 2003. http://www.harrisinteractive.com/harris_poll.

Helgesen, Sally. 1990. *The Female Advantage: Women's Ways of Leadership*. New York: Doubleday.

———. 1995. *The Web of Inclusion: A New Architecture for Building Great Organizations*. New York: Currency/Doubleday.

Hesselbein, Frances. 2002. "The Key to Cultural Transformation," In *On Leading Change*, edited by Frances Hesselbein and Rob Johnston, pp. 1–5. San Francisco: Jossey-Bass.

Hesselbein, Frances, and Rob Johnston. 2002a. *On Creativity, Innovation, and Renewal*. San Francisco: Jossey-Bass.

———, eds. 2002b. *On Leading Change: A Leader to Leader Guide*. San Francisco: Jossey-Bass.

*Holy Bible*. 1950. King James Version. Philadelphia: A.J. Holman.

Horowitz, David. 2002. "Missing Diversity on America's Campuses." http://www.frontpagemag.com/articles/readarticle.asp?ID = 1003.

Horrigan, John, et. al. 2003. *The Ever-Shifting Internet Population: A New Look at Internet Access and the Digital Divide*. Washington, D.C.: Pew Internet and American Life Project.

Ikenberry, Stanley O. 1998. "From Our President." *The Presidency* 1, no. 2: 5–6.

Ingraham, M.H. 1968. *The Mirror of Brass: The Compensation and Working Conditions of College and University Administrators*. Madison, Wis.: University of Wisconsin.

Jones, Del. 2003. "Few Women Hold Top Executive Jobs, Even When CEOs Are Female." *USA Today*, 27 January, B01–2.

Kelly, R.M. 1991. *The Gendered Economy: Work Careers, and Success*. Newbury Park, Calif.: Sage Publications.

Kerr, Clark. 1972. *The Uses of the University*. Cambridge, Mass.: Harvard University Press.

———. 1984. *Presidents Make a Difference*. New York: Carnegie Corporation.

Kipnis, D. 1976. *The Powerholders*. Chicago: University of Chicago.

Knight, Frank H. 1921. *Risk, Uncertainty and Profit*. Boston: Houghton-Mifflin.

Koch, James V. 2003. "TQM and Other Management Fads: Why Has Their Impact on Higher Education Been So Small?" Twenty-Second David Dodds Henry Lecture. Champaign-Urbana, Ill.: University of Illinois.

Kosmin, Barry A., and Egon Mayer. 2001. *American Religious Identification Survey, 2001*. New York: Graduate Center of the City University of New York.

Levine, Arthur (ed.). 1993. *Higher Learning in America, 1980–2000*. Baltimore: Johns Hopkins.

Maletz, Mark C., and Jon R. Katzenbach. 2002. "Reinventing Management Development." In *On Leading Change*, edited by Frances Hesselbein and Rob Johnston, pp. 115–26. San Francisco: Jossey-Bass.

March, James G. 1980. "How We Talk and How We Act: Administrative Theory and Administrative Life." Seventh David Dodds Henry Lecture. Champaign-Urbana, Ill.: University of Illinois.

Marginson, Simon, and Mark Considine. 2000. *Enterprise University: Power, Governance and Reinvention in Australia.* Cambridge: Cambridge University Press.

Marshall, Helen E. 1956. *Grandest of Enterprises.* Normal, Ill.: Illinois State University.

Mathews, Jay. 2001. "It's Lowly at the Top: What Became of the Great College Presidents?" *Washington Post,* 10 June, B01.

Mayhew, Lewis B. 1979. *Surviving the Eighties.* San Francisco: Jossey-Bass.

McFarlin, Charles H., Barbara J. Crittenden, and Larry H. Ebbers. 1999. "Background Factors Common Among Outstanding Community College Presidents." *Community College Review* 27 (Winter): 19–32.

*Merriam-Webster Unabridged Dictionary.* 2003. Electronic version. http://www.odu.edu.

Milwid, Beth. 1990. *Working with Men.* Hillsboro, Ore.: Beyond Words Publishing.

Mintzberg, Henry. 1975. "The Manager's Job: Folklore and Fact." *Harvard Business Review* 53, no. 4: 49–61.

Morley, Jay, and Doug Eadie. 2001. *The Extraordinary Higher Education Leader.* Washington, D.C.: National Association of College and University Business Officers.

Morrison, Anne M., and Mary Ann Van Glinow. 1990. "Women and Minorities in Management." *American Psychologist* 45 (February): 200–208.

Naisbitt, John, and Patricia Auberdene. 1992. *Reinventing the Corporation.* New York: Warner Books.

National Science Foundation. 2003. *Academic Research and Development Expenditures: Fiscal Year 2001.* Washington, D.C.: National Science Foundation.

*Oxford English Dictionary, Second Edition.* 2003. Electronic Version. http://www.odu.edu.

Peck, Robert D. 1983. "The Entrepreneurial College Presidency." *Educational Record* 64 (Winter): 18–25.

Peter, Lawrence J. 1977. *Peter's Quotations: Ideas for Our Time.* New York: Bantam Books.

Pew Internet and American Life Project. 2003. *America's Online Pursuits: The Changing Picture of Who's Online and What They Do.* Washington, D.C.: Pew Internet and American Life Project.

Plowman, Rodney J. 1991. "Perceptions of Presidential Leadership Behavior and Institutional Environment by Presidents and Vice Presidents of Selected Four-Year Colleges and Universities in Florida." Unpublished doctoral dissertation, School of Education, University of Mississippi, Oxford, Miss.

Posner, Barry Z., and James M. Kouzes. 1993. "Psychometric Properties of the Leadership Practices Inventory—Updated." *Educational and Psychological Measurement* 53 (Spring): 191–99.

Pruitt, George. 1974. "Blueprint for Leadership: The American College Presidency." Unpublished doctoral dissertation, Union for Experimenting Colleges and Universities, Cincinnati, Ohio.

Rodenhouse, Mary Pat. 2001. *2002 Higher Education Directory*. Falls Church, Va.: Higher Education Publications.

Schumpeter, Joseph. 1923. *The Theory of Economic Development*. Cambridge, Mass.: Harvard University Press.

Sellers, Patricia. 2002. "The New Breed." *Fortune* 146 (18 November): 66 ff.

Shaw, Kenneth A. 1999. *The Successful President: "BuzzWords" on Leadership*. Phoenix, Ariz.: Oryx/ACE.

Tomek, William G. 1993. "Confirmation and Replication in Empirical Econometrics: A Step Toward Improved Scholarship." *American Journal of Agricultural Economics* 75 (October): 6–14.

U.S. Census Bureau. 2003a. http://www.census.gov/main/www/cen2000.html.

———. 2003b. http://www.census.gov/prod/www/statistical-abstract-02.html.

Useem, Jerry. 2002. "Tyrants, Statesmen, and Destroyers." *Fortune*, 18 November, 82–84 ff.

Veblen, Thorstein. 1918. *The Higher Learning in America: A Memorandum on the Conduct of Universities by Business Men*. New York: Viking Press.

Vroom, Victor H. 1983. "Leaders and Leadership in Academe." *Review of Higher Education* 6 (Summer): 367–86.

Walker, Donald E. 1979. *The Effective Administrator: A Practical Approach to Problem Solving, Decision Making, and Campus Leadership*. San Francisco: Jossey-Bass.

Weinstein, Laurence A. 1993. *Moving a Battleship with Your Bare Hands: Governing a University System*. Madison, Wis.: Magna.

West, C., and D. Zimmerman. 1991. "Doing Gender." In *The Social Construction of Gender*. Newbury Park, Calif.: Sage Publications.

Whetten, D.A. 1984. "Effective Campus Administrators: Good Management on Campus." *Change* 16, no. 8: 38–43.

Wright, Jeanette T. 1988. "Conditions for Effectiveness." In *Leaders on Leadership: The College Presidency*, edited by James L. Fisher and Martha W. Tack, pp. 87–91. San Francisco: Jossey-Bass.

# Index

## About the Authors

JAMES L. FISHER holds a Ph.D. in psychology from Northwestern University. He is President Emeritus of the Council for Advancement & Support of Education (CASE) and President Emeritus of Towson University. He is presently Professor of Leadership Studies at the Union Institute and University and a consultant to boards and presidents. He has taught at Northwestern, Illinois State, Johns Hopkins, Harvard, and has been a consultant to more than 300 colleges and universities. He is one of the most published writers in higher education today. He has been published in *The New York Times*, *The Washington Times*, and *The Baltimore Sun*. The author or editor of nine books, his book, *The Power of the Presidency*, was reviewed in Change magazine as "The most important book ever written on the college presidency" and was nominated for the nonfiction Pulitzer Prize.

JAMES V. KOCH is Board of Visitors Professor of Economics and President Emeritus at Old Dominion University. He has also held teaching and research positions at institutions including Illinois State University, the University of Grenoble (France), Brown University, the University of Montana, the University of Hawaii, and the Royal Melbourne Institute of Technology in Australia. He served as President of the University of Montana (1986-1990) and Old Dominion University (1990-2001) and has served as an advisor to more than 60 corporations, governing boards, and college presidents.